W9-ABY-690

Advance praise for *Walk Softly and Carry a Great Bag*

"One of Teresa's greatest gifts is her uncanny ability to present a perfect combination of reality and spirituality, and this book touches the hearts and concerns of women in every stage of life, no matter what their circumstances. With all that women do these days, *Walk Softly* is a "must-have"—the practical thoughts and prayers guide readers to a deeper relationship with God. Whether you read it in the car-pool line, while waiting in the doctor's office, during Adoration, or at the end of the day before getting ready for bed, Teresa's words will speak to your heart and the prayers will move you."

—JULIE ALEXANDER, cofounder, the Alexander House,
and coauthor, *Marriage 911*

"*Walk Softly and Carry a Great Bag* is just what the doctor ordered—it's precisely what every Christian woman today needs in her bag or on her night table. Teresa brings womanly insight, Catholic teaching, humor, and a whole lot of love into this modern-day devotional. I absolutely love this book!"

—DONNA-MARIE COOPER O'BOYLE, EWTN TV host,
award-winning author, *The Miraculous Medal*

"Who says you can't have style with your time with God? Teresa Tomeo finds a way to make on-the-go devotions more than just a passing fad, and she does it with style and verve. This is a book you can tuck in your bag, share with your best friend, and use to grow closer to God."

—SARAH REINHARD, author and blogger

"*Walk Softly and Carry a Great Bag* reminds me daily to ask for help, take care of myself, and appreciate all God has given me."

—CARY ALFONSO

"Teresa Tomeo has done it again! Inspirational and entertaining at the same time, *Walk Softly and Carry a Great Bag* is a down-to-earth and eminently practical guide for today's hyper-busy woman. Would you like to know the secret of how to transform the distractions of everyday life into opportunities for spiritual growth? Then get this book!"

—MARCELLINO D'AMBROSIO ("Dr. Italy"), author, *When the Church Was Young*

"*Walk Softly and Carry a Great Bag* is classic Teresa Tomeo: In her customary Italian style, she tells it like it is, reminding us that God loves a modern woman, and that a modern woman needs to spend time with God, no matter how chaotic her life might feel. In this book you'll find practical spiritual advice that a busy woman can consume in just a few minutes but process for the rest of the day. It's a perfect book to keep next to the makeup mirror to read while getting ready…or in your purse for whenever you find a few precious moments for reflection on the go!"

—ANNA MITCHELL, news director and producer,
EWTN Radio *Son Rise Morning Show*

"This delightful little book combines the wisdom of the saints with the sassy wit of a close girlfriend. The entries are brief, powerful, and often funny—just what the modern Catholic woman needs to give her spiritual life a boost."

—JENNIFER FULWILER, radio host and author, *Something Other Than God*

"Carry a great bag…big enough to fit this book, because once you pick it up, you won't want to put it down! With wit and wisdom, Teresa Tomeo offers the busiest woman a quick (and I do mean quick) way to take "me" time, and with simple devotions that refuel and refresh, she shows how true happiness resides in letting every single aspect of your life be accompanied by the Lord.

—KELLY WAHLQUIST, author, *Created to Relate*

"Like sitting down for a pep talk over cappuccino with a trusted friend, *Walk Softly and Carry a Great Bag* is a little luxury, a timely gift you deserve to give yourself in the midst of life's busyness and stress. Teresa Tomeo's wit, wisdom, and beautiful soul permeate these pages. This daily devotional delivers a boost to get you revved up to give your very best to God and the world around you. Toss it in your best bag, pray with it daily, and live life to the fullest!"

—Lisa M. Hendey, founder of CatholicMom.com and author, *The Grace of Yes*

"As someone who has struggled with anxiety for most of my life, I know the power of letting God speak to me through pages of the Bible. Unfortunately, many people are too busy or too unfamiliar with Scripture to tap into this great resource. In *Walk Softly and Carry a Great Bag*, Teresa Tomeo makes it practical for anyone to obtain a quick biblical boost whenever necessary! Each verse is personalized with an uplifting reflection—it's perfect for those who 'don't have time' to read the Bible. Highly recommended!"

—Gary Zimak, Catholic speaker and author, *Faith, Hope, and Clarity*

"Like the Martha Stewart of Catholic womanhood, Teresa Tomeo knows how to pull it all together. Faithful, funny, and a little feisty, Teresa's reflections are a treat for any woman who wants a bite-sized daily morsel to spice up her spiritual routine."

—Gina Loehr, author, *St. Francis, Pope Francis*

"An old adage in the spiritual life says that if the devil can't make you bad, he'll make you busy. Teresa Tomeo has written useful short reflections that busy people can carry with them for personal prayer and spiritual growth. Put it in your bag!"

—Fr. Mitch Pacwa, S.J., EWTN host and author,
The Holy Land: An Armchair Pilgrimage

"Once again Teresa combines her trademark wit and substance that pierces the heart and draws us closer to God. This year, I'm going to begin my days with *Walk Softly*. Bravo!"

—MEG MEEKER, M.D, author, *Strong Mothers, Strong Sons*

"How much do I love this devotional? Lots! What kind of woman would benefit from having a copy of this in her purse? Every kind! In typical Teresa Tomeo style, *Walk Softly and Carry a Great Bag* offers humor, joy, inspiration, and a reality check with bite-sized stories, gentle admonishments, timely reminders, and humble prayers. This book covers a wide range of issues women from all walks of life encounter in their lives; it's a joyful jumble of God, friends, family, work, dinner plans, child care, housework, and lipstick. Tomeo's pithy writing will have you laughing out loud, reflecting thoughtfully, and praying with your whole heart, sometimes all on the same page!"

—DANIELLE BEAN, author, *Momnipotent*

Walk Softly and Carry a Great Bag
On-the-Go Devotions

TERESA TOMEO

servant

AN IMPRINT OF
FRANCISCAN MEDIA
Cincinnati, Ohio

Scripture passages have been taken from the *Revised Standard Version*, Catholic edition. Copyright 1946, 1952, 1971 by the Division of Christian Education of the National Council of Churches of Christ in the USA. Used by permission. All rights reserved. Quotes are taken from the English translation of the *Catechism of the Catholic Church* for the United States of America (indicated as *CCC*), 2nd ed. Copyright 1997 by United States Catholic Conference—Libreria Editrice Vaticana.

LIBRARY OF CONGRESS CATALOGING-IN-PUBLICATION DATA
Tomeo, Teresa.
Walk softly and carry a great bag / Teresa Tomeo.
pages cm
Includes bibliographical references.
ISBN 978-1-61636-882-1 (alk. paper)
1. Catholic women—Prayers and devotions. 2. Catholic women—Religious life. I. Title.
BX2170.W7T66 2015
248.8'43—dc23
2014046801

ISBN 978-1-61636-882-1

Published by Servant, an imprint of Franciscan Media
28 W. Liberty St.
Cincinnati, OH 45202
www.FranciscanMedia.org

Printed in the United States of America.
Printed on acid-free paper.
15 16 17 18 19 5 4 3 2 1

Contents

Introduction

So what's in your bag? Hmm, let's see…lipstick, sunglasses, some old chewing gum, keys, of course your cell phone, some crumpled Kleenex—and hopefully now this devotional. That's the idea anyway: a devotional book that fits nicely in your favorite bag or briefcase—a devotional that will also hopefully fit into a corner of your heart. Think of this as your go-to inspiration for women on the go, helping you deal with a variety of life's challenging issues from a Christian perspective.

Regardless of your state in life, no doubt you're busy, just as we all are. That means not too many of us have the time or the luxury to read St. Augustine's *Confessions* or the Bible from cover to cover, but we're still looking for guidance in so many areas of our life. We look for guidance in all areas—relationships, time management, finances, challenges at home and in the workplace, along with one of the biggest challenges today: the constant and often confusing messages from the culture.

As far as this book is concerned, it's probably a lot like your purse: just about everything you need is in there. The idea is to carry this devotional with you as you carry that bag. That way, when you have a few minutes, before going to bed or maybe on your lunch break, you can pick up *Walk Softly*. If you have a question about some aspect of faith or a particular challenge you're facing, I hope you'll find some instruction from the Lord along with some peace of mind in these pages.

Today's modern American woman is the queen of multitasking—juggling, jobs, children's homework, housework, church commitments, social commitments…you name it. You probably consider it a good day if you actually have time to read a few ingredients on the back of the cereal box. You get the picture…and that is exactly why I wrote this book. We're all busy. But deep down we also know that none of what we do really matters if we're not rooted in something or someone much bigger than ourselves.

Our often toxic and increasingly secular society tells us just the opposite—that we no longer need anybody, and we certainly don't need God. We can figure out this thing called life on our own. It's not really that complicated, because we just live from one experience to the next. Whether it's the promotion, the weekend in Vegas with your BFF, splurging on that new top, or finding a new boy toy, it's all about you. That said, if you're reading this book, then you're one of the smart ladies who has realized that a life revolving around "me, myself, and I" can get lonely pretty quickly. Benedict XVI hit the nail on the head a few years ago when he addressed a Vatican women's conference in 2008, which I was privileged to attend.

When, therefore, men or women pretend to be autonomous or totally self-sufficient, they risk being closed up in a self-realization that considers the overcoming of every natural, social or religious bond as a conquest of freedom, but which in fact reduces them to an oppressive solitude. To foster and support the true promotion of women and men one cannot fail to take this reality into account.[1]

What the world is selling women is a big, fat bill of goods. Deep down you're looking for something more. But at the same time, you're trying to figure out how to fit that "something more" in to an already crazy, hectic life and an already stuffed-to-the-gills handbag.

Maybe you've already come a long way in your journey with Jesus and just want a daily spiritual pick-me-up, a dose of good news—*the* Good News actually—to encourage you, to keep you grounded or perhaps to motivate you to dig a little deeper. Maybe you are just making your way back into the arms of Christ. Whatever your particular situation, you've come to the right place because *Walk Softly* is designed to fit into any size purse as well as any lifestyle, no matter where you are at in your faith.

Hopefully you'll laugh along with me as I poke fun at myself (which is such an easy thing to do). I'll share some of what I have learned in my own faith experience, but you'll also see how God is far from finished with me yet. I am definitely still a major, and I mean major, work in progress. For example, while I share a lot of ideas on slowing down, this is still a huge challenge for me. And while media influence is a particular area of expertise for me, believe it or not, I am also am still impacted by the media in many ways—particularly when I look in the mirror.

In addition to sharing insight on a variety of issues, along with some commentary for personal reflection, *Walk Softly* also provides you with a daily prayer related to the topic. If you're not praying on a regular basis, these meditations might jump start your prayer life. If you're a regular prayer warrior, you too will feel right at home and will be encouraged to keep going.

It is also my sincere hope that this book—in a loving way, of course—just might give you that little kick in the rear we all need from time to time to help us refocus and get us back on the right track. So grab that great bag of yours; get ready to head out the door and take no prisoners, but not without taking this devotional with you. Here's hoping and praying *Walk Softly* will lighten your load and put a little more spring in your step.

God Is in the Details

And surely I am with you always, until the end of the age.
—MATTHEW 28:20

It really gets my Italian up when I hear people say, "The devil is in the details." Actually it is *God* who is in the details. He wants to be with us in every area of our lives—the big stuff, the small stuff, the good, the bad, and the ugly, so to speak, right in the midst of our hectic, everyday lives. You will find that by taking a moment to pray to him, to think about him and how much he loves you, he will reveal himself to you. He will acknowledge you acknowledging him—and in some pretty unexpected ways. We serve a very detailed God. Each of us, however, has to be open.

Let me give you one lovely example of how the Lord is indeed right there with us every day as we go about our business. My husband and I were busy getting our backyard and patio ready for the coming summer season. It was a Saturday afternoon, and the nursery was the last store on the shopping agenda that day. My husband is the one with green thumb, so when we visit the home-and-garden-type stores, he takes off with his list, and I tend to wander around, just looking at all the lovely plants and flowers.

That is exactly what I was doing when I had my "God moment."

Now, I can barely tell a petunia from a peony, but I do know beauty when I see it. This particular day, browsing in that nursery in suburban Detroit, I was stunned at God's glory. There are just so many different varieties of plant life and so many different shapes and sizes. The vibrant colors alone took my breath away. And then, suddenly I heard a Catholic hymn playing overhead. Background music in shops and malls is commonplace these days, but Schubert's "Ave Maria"? Even the most skeptical among us would have to find that selection interesting, to say the least. For Catholic Christians this hymn carries particular significance because of the Blessed Mother's association with flowers (in particular roses). As the hymn played I happened to be standing in the middle of two aisles filled with yellow, pink, and white, rosebushes, along with a kaleidoscope of other fragrant flowers. I immediately felt a tug on my heart (which skipped a few beats). I truly felt this was God's way of acknowledging my praises.

So remember: God is in the details. Where will you find him today? Remember he is with us always—even at your local nursery.

Pray Softly...

As I go about my daily routine, Lord, please open my eyes and my heart to see your glory. Remind me that you are in every detail of our lives, no matter how small or ordinary.

Don't Just Do Something—Sit There

Be still and know that I am God.
—Psalm 46:10

Seriously? Yes, seriously—and quite seriously, as a matter of fact. After all, we can't give what we don't have, and how many of us feel like we just don't have much left at the end of the day? We look like a bunch of gerbils spinning around and around on the wheel in their cage, getting nowhere fast. Sometimes I feel like screaming, "Stop the world! I want to get off," don't you? How many of us can identify with the mom in that old Calgon commercial. You know the one, where the woman is in the middle of the TV screen and there are images of crying children, a cranky boss, and dirty dishes swimming around her heart. Suddenly she cries out, "Calgon, take me away!" In the next scene, we see her relaxing in a luxurious tub filled with soap bubbles, looking very peaceful and serene. Oh, to be her for a day—or even an afternoon.

That commercial hit the airwaves in the early 80s. Women have always been busy bees. But it's probably not a stretch to say that we are busier now than we have ever been. For a variety of reasons, women have taken on more responsibility—sometimes at home, sometimes in the workplace, or both. That's not necessarily a bad thing, unless a woman somehow loses herself in the process. Our nurturing nature makes us prone to putting ourselves last on the list, and if we're not careful, this can damage us physically, emotionally, and spiritually.

Maybe because of all those daily responsibilities with family and/ or career, taking a two-hour siesta or a leisurely bath is not anywhere in your foreseeable future—and that's OK. Maybe you'd love to do a weekend retreat, but that's not on the radar screen either, given the demands on your plate. That doesn't mean you can't slip off for a few grace-filled moments to be with the Lord. It's all the more reason to "be still" and just "sit there." This can be at your desk. It can be in the back of the bus on the way home from work or at home in the morning before everyone else wakes up. But wherever or whenever, just be still and know that God is God.

Pray softly...

Dear Lord, help me slow down today, even just for a few minutes. Let me start and end each day by giving it to you and offering all my responsibilities, commitments, and tasks for the glory of your kingdom. Remind me that the world will not end if I take a break from the hustle and bustle to be with you. It might even be a better place, because every moment with you makes me a better person.

Don't Pray for a Lighter Load, Just a Bigger Bag

My yoke is easy and my burden light.
—MATTHEW 11:30

Mother Teresa once wrote: "Do not think that my spiritual life is strewn with roses—that is the flower which I hardly ever find on my way. Quite the contrary, I have more often as my companion 'darkness.'"[2] Yes, Blessed Mother Teresa—the winner of the Nobel Peace Prize, and a woman who is sure to be a saint in the near future. She, too, at times felt overburdened with her tasks at hand. She, too, had her own "dark night of the soul." Her dark night actually lasted for years, but she kept on keeping on and never turned her back on the poorest of the poor in the slums of India and many other places around the world.

Another great saint, the much loved and well known mystic and Doctor of the Catholic Church, St. Teresa of Avila, was also known to speak directly to the Lord about the trials and tribulations she faced as she went about Spain trying to reform the Carmelite order. It is said that during one particularly rough time when she was traveling cross-country in a horse-drawn wagon, she ran into some extremely rough terrain and even rougher weather. The wagon turned over and a very frustrated Teresa looked up at the heavens and blurted out, "Lord, if this is the way you treat your friends, no wonder you have so few of them."[3]

So take heart. If you're having a bad day, a bad week, or even a bad year, you're in good company—especially if you think about Jesus himself. Think about him sweating blood in the Garden of Gethsemane. "My Father, if you are willing, remove this chalice from me; nevertheless not my will, but yours, be done" (Luke 22:42).

So if Jesus and some of his most well-known witnesses have cried out to God the Father about the weight of the world on their shoulders, you can be sure you're not alone. This doesn't give you and me the right to go on with our perpetual pity party. Jesus didn't quit and neither did Blessed Mother Teresa or St. Teresa of Avila. Jesus' death on the cross resulted in the salvation of the world. Mother Teresa saved lives and comforted and fed thousands more. St. Teresa of Avila not only reformed the Carmelite order but her deep spiritual writings transformed the practice of personal prayer and communion with Christ. It does mean that we should be calling on the Lord to ask us for his help in completing the tasks to which we have been assigned, whether inside the home, outside the home or both. Sharing your thoughts and feelings about your situation with God can indeed lighten that burden.

OK, we know that Jesus is King of kings and Lord of lords. And very few of us are ever going to even come close to being in the same league as Mother Teresa and St. Teresa. But we are called to emulate them and to do our best to carry our burdens *and* learn from them. But here is something else to think about: Jesus called the disciples to help carry out his mission here on earth. Mother Teresa, St. Teresa, and other great teachers didn't carry out their work alone, and neither do our popes, bishops, pastors, and priests. They learned to delegate. So, if you're carrying too heavy of a load, you might want to look around your home or the office and see where some of the weight might need to be distributed. Oftentimes we women think we have to be everything to everybody 24/7. Remember that it's OK to ask not only for a bigger purse (as in the strength to handle your responsibilities as well as challenges), but also for some others to join in the lifting.

Pray softly...

Dear Lord, help carry my burdens today with arms open wide, using my responsibilities, as well as my problems or challenges, as a chance to get closer to you. Help me to admit when I have taken on too much and for the ability to ask not only for your help, but also for the help of others.

Life Is What Happens When You're Busy Making Other Plans...and Dinner

Rejoice always, pray constantly, give thanks in all circumstances;
for this is the will of God in Christ Jesus for you.
—1 Thessalonians 5:16–18

What in the world happened? You ask yourself this question as you're rushing from work to pick up the kids from school or you're standing in the checkout line at the local supermarket trying to figure out if you'll have time to throw dinner together before the baseball or soccer game. By now you were supposed to have sipped champagne in the shadow of the Eiffel Tower, hiked through the Alps, and floated along the canals of Venice in a lovely gondola. Maybe instead of world travel, you had your sights on soaring up the corporate ladder at breakneck speed, taking no prisoners and shattering all kinds of company records for earnings in your chosen profession. So how did you go from dreams of grandeur to what seems like just an ordinary everyday life? How come the closest you're going to get to exotic or exciting now seems to be the imported fruit aisle at the local health food store? How did life pass you by? Whatever your place in life, you're keenly aware now more than ever you're not where you thought you'd be.

I get it. After all, if you told me I would be in Catholic media writing and speaking about faith issues instead of on the local news talking about the latest three-alarm fire or crooked politician, I would have told you that you were a few sandwiches short of a picnic. This isn't where I was supposed to end up. But I have come to realize that, not only is it where I am supposed to be, it's where I want to be and where I am the happiest and most fulfilled I have ever been. Do I ever wonder what it would be like if I were still an anchorwoman for the local evening news? Sure—but I don't have any regrets. As a matter of fact, given the sorry state of the news business, I continually thank God for taking me out of that hectic, hedonistic environment, even though he had to do it with me kicking and screaming. I'm eternally grateful he gave me a whole new mission and career, along with a much more peaceful and sane environment.

So don't be too quick to discount where you are right now. It doesn't mean you're not ever going to travel to that far-off place someday. You still might be the next biggest thing to hit Wall Street, Madison Avenue, or the Via Veneto. It does mean, however, that you need to take a fresh look at where God has planted you—and why. It's also a reminder to learn to appreciate the countless gifts he has given you, especially those that have come to you unexpectedly. Don't let yourself get too busy questioning why things happened a certain way, or you're liable to miss the beauty and sacredness of it all. You might be surrounded by pots and the pans, but if you look, you'll find God right there with you. And don't forget what Dorothy said after she finally made her way back to Kansas, "If I ever go looking for my heart's desire again, I won't look any further than my own backyard. Because if it isn't there, I never really lost it to begin with!"[4]

Pray softly...

Dear Lord, help me to bloom where I am planted—even if where I am planted isn't where I thought I would be at this point in my life. Help me make the most of every day and to see how your plan is always the best plan for me.

Put One Foot in Front of the Other, But Don't Forget the Pedicure

You are altogether beautiful, my friend,
there is no flaw in you.
—Song of Songs 4:7, *NAB*

"Wearing makeup is an act of charity." I burst out laughing when I heard a good friend of mine, a fellow Christian speaker, blurt this out at a women's retreat. But how true is it really? If we are going to be the best we can be for the Lord, our families, and ourselves, where did we ever get the idea that being faithful translates into frumpy? What would you think if a woman showed up at your office to conduct a business seminar or at your local church to lead a retreat wearing dirty sweatpants and a T-shirt? I don't know about you, but one obvious conclusion might be that she doesn't care about herself or isn't too interested in those to whom she is presenting. If our bodies are temples of the Holy Spirit, why do some treat them like Dumpsters?

Since these are devotions for busy women on the go, I'm not suggesting that you spend hours each week at the salon getting all dolled up. Who has the time or the money for that kind of beauty regimen—especially if you're juggling a job and a family? But you'll feel much better about yourself when you do start treating your body as a temple. We women, however, are so busy taking care of everyone else that we sometimes forget—or even feel guilty—about doing more than just pulling our hair back in a scrunchie and throwing on some drugstore lipstick.

Getting back to my friend's hysterical (but oh-so-true) comment on makeup, think about the kind of impression you can have if you are trying to connect as a Christian woman with other women in the world. Yes, we're called to be in the world but not *of* the world. But what does it say about the Christian life if we regularly look like something the cat just dragged in? For the answer to that question, let me repeat something said during a group discussion at a women's retreat I was giving in Kansas City, Kansas. I was speaking to a group of women whose husbands were studying to be deacons in the Catholic Church. I explained that, in my role as a public person, I have to be aware of what I look like every time I walk out the door. It's a bit more intense in my case because I have been on radio and TV since dirt and am a recognizable face, particularly in my hometown of Detroit. However, I explained to the ladies that once their husbands were ordained, they also would be under the microscope. They would be seen as leaders and pillars in their church community, so presenting themselves in a professional and attractive manner would be even more important. For me this has become a double whammy since, in addition to being a public person in the media, my husband is also a deacon.

Some of the women disagreed, insisting that it is all about what's on the inside that really counts. While that's true, another women chimed in, saying that a bad first impression can easily steer someone away from going deeper or getting to know more about you and your beliefs—in other words, what's on the inside.

"I am a homeschooling mom, and I work in the pro-life movement. I attend a lot of church-related events," she said. "If I show up looking sloppy and disheveled, who would to listen to what I have to say?"

Bingo and brava! Now pick up the phone and go get that pedi!

Pray softly...

Dear Lord, help me to remember that putting my best foot forward for you means taking care of the outside as well as the inside. Help me to apply moderation when it comes to addressing my appearance—show me how not to be overly focused on outward beauty but to be able to treat my body as a temple of the Holy Spirit.

I Am Woman: Hear Me Snore!

And on the seventh day God finished his work that he had done,
and he rested on the seventh day from all his work that he had done.
—GENESIS 2:2–3

"I'm just so tired." "I am just too busy." These are the two statements I hear the most from women when the subject of becoming more active in their faith life comes up. Thanks in a big way to radical feminism and other cultural messages convincing us that we can and must do it all and have it all, we see ourselves as wonder women and don't rest nearly enough (if at all).

I want to take a moment to speak to the career women reading this book. Don't do what I did and listen to the voices of the culture telling you that it is all about the work. Been there. Done that. Bought the T-shirt, as the old saying goes. I also bought the lies, and those lies almost cost me, as I explain in detail when I give my personal testimony, not only my marriage, but my very soul.

My previous business, the news business, is one of those 24/7 gigs that never sleeps, and for a long time neither did I, almost literally. That's what I was told had to happen in order to "make it" in the news business. Working long hours—weekends, nights, early mornings—and never saying no to being called at any hour to cover a breaking story were supposedly the building blocks for gaining and maintaining a top spot on the air waves. Unfortunately that same attitude is taken as the norm when it comes to women in many of today's professions. It is a mindset perpetuated by feminists as outlined in a refreshingly honest article, "Why Women Still Can't Have It All," written by a former member of the Obama administration, Anne-Marie Slaughter. She had reached the top of her profession, becoming the first woman policy director at the State Department, but she was increasingly troubled by the long periods of time spent away from her family. She was supposed to be the poster child for the woman who has it all, but she started to feel like she had gotten it all wrong…and so had the feminist movement.

> I was increasingly aware that the feminist beliefs on which I had built my entire career were shifting under my feet. I had always assumed that if I could get a foreign-policy job in the State Department or the White House while my party was in power, I would stay the course as long as I had the opportunity to do work I loved. But in January 2011, when my two-year public-service leave from Princeton University was up, I hurried home as fast as I could.[5]

Both Anne-Marie Slaughter and I learned the hard way: Women still can't have it all. Something is going to give, so give yourself a rest. That doesn't necessarily mean you have to change careers or stay home full-time. It does mean you need to put some balance back in your life before your life is spinning out of control. I gave up countless evenings, weekends, and holidays with my husband and family in order to "get ahead." I figured the marriage could take care of itself and that my husband and I could build our relationship around "quality time" together. God wasn't even in the picture. How could he be? Where would he fit in to my rat race lifestyle? It took me way too long to discover that the business I sacrificed so much for thought little about sacrificing me. When I finally woke up and smelled the cappuccino, my life was just about in shambles all around me.

If I had taken the time to rest and build some balance along the way, I would have been much better off. So set some healthy boundaries for yourself when it comes to your workload. Give yourself and your family a break and make room for God. Your job will still be there on Monday—and who knows you might even be a source of inspiration for other working gals to follow in your footsteps.

Pray softly...

Dear Lord, I want to be more like you and learn to rest after a hard day's work. Help me to be strong and resist the temptation to put work before faith and family. Teach me to rest in the knowledge that you are in control and the world will go on without me taking that phone call.

All I Want for Christmas Is a Good Night's Sleep

In peace I will both lie down and sleep;
for you alone, O Lord, make me dwell in safety.

—PSALM 4:8

What a hypocrite! No getting around that. There I was, giving an Advent reflection about slowing down during the Advent season and at the same time doing a really bad job of practicing what I was preaching. Instead of slowing down, my pace during the holidays that year kept picking up. "Oh, sure, I can do that talk for you, Father." "Oh, no problem. I will host Christmas this year." "Of course I'll run to the mall yet again and get all those last few items for family, friends, and charity."

The ladies at the Advent Tea were impressed with my talk. It sounded good, it looked good on paper and in my Power Point presentation, but it wasn't anywhere near real life for me. As a result, by the time Christmas rolled around, all I wanted to do was sleep.

It's nothing new to hear about the importance of slowing down during the holidays. But let this be yet another reminder to take a breather. Put the Wonder Woman costume away this year, and learn to delegate. You really don't have to make all those cookies yourself. You really can ask relatives to bring a side dish or a desert. And you really can skip one, two, or maybe even three parties or get-togethers and stay home. Or you can learn the hard way, as my husband and I did.

It was Thanksgiving weekend 2010. The weather was mild, and so my husband and I set out to accomplish many a task on our very long holiday to-do list. We began by decorating our home. He would handle the outdoor lights, and I would get to work on the inside. Once that was accomplished, we would be off to the mall to start tackling the shopping list, and after that maybe we would even manage to bake a few dozen cookies before the weekend was over.

That plan was nice while it lasted, but it didn't last very long. As my husband was attempting to string the lights on one of our trees in the front yard, somehow the ladder gave way and he went crashing to the ground, landing on the cement drive way. His right arm literally broke his fall. Thank the good Lord, he did not hit his head on the cement, but he did shatter his right wrist—as well as most of our Christmas activities. His injury required major surgery along with major rest. So much for the office parties, the baking, and the entertaining. We ended up spending most of that Advent and Christmas at home in front of the fire with a glass of wine. It turned out to be one of the best Christmas seasons of our lives, but it took a broken wrist to get our attention. Hopefully I've grabbed yours.

Pray softly...

Dear Lord, please help me realize that you truly are the real reason for all of the seasons. Let me make the most of the holy days and holidays, but let me also see every day as a gift from you.

Spare the iPod—Don't Spoil the Child

Fathers, do not provoke your children to anger,
but bring them up in the discipline and instruction of the Lord.
—Ephesians 6:4

A few toys I received growing up were really near to my heart, including a musical teddy bear my father bought for me while he was still serving in the Merchant Marines. There was also the dollhouse he put together—or should I say tried to put together—one Christmas morning. It is not so much the items themselves but the memories and gestures attached to them that made those toys priceless.

Growing up in the 60s and 70s, I didn't feel deprived. We were a middle-class family, and I thought I was pretty lucky to receive what seemed at the time some pretty cool stuff. But outside of those two toys, the rest of the gifts I just don't remember. You probably have similar experiences, because when push comes to shove, material things are nice while they last, but they don't last long. The thrill is gone pretty quickly.

That's why it is so sad when parents tell me (and they do quite often) that they simply have to make sure their kids have it so much better materially than they did growing up. Most of the people I know who are my age, at the tail end of the baby boomer generation, grew up in a middle class family like mine. We weren't rich, but we didn't exactly walk to school through the snow in bare feet because our parents couldn't to buy us shoes. Having to actually get up and walk over to the TV to turn the channel does not constitute great suffering. Maybe it was the one TV in the house combined with the lack of a remote that did them in. But honestly, in general most of us still had it pretty good. So why all the melodrama when it comes to saying no to little Sally or Sammy when they bug Mommy and Daddy for the brand-new, fully loaded iPhone? And yes, at my media awareness seminars, I have actually had moms ask me how to say no to their own children. The huge pressure from the advertising industry doesn't help, nor does the fact that most parents want their children's approval. Interestingly enough there is a growing body of evidence that teaching kids to live more like St. Francis and less like the Paris Hilton is what really makes them happy. Go figure.

A 2012 study by University of British Columbia psychologists found that children are actually happier to give than to receive. The lead author, Lara Akin, said the toddlers involved in the study were asked to give away their own treats and their extra treats without a single child throwing themselves on the floor kicking and screaming.[6] Imagine that.

Spending time volunteering, making donations, or sharing resources with others all lead to happiness. What a concept! Where have we heard those words of wisdom before? You already know the answer. Now go and do likewise. Give your kids more memories and less stuff. Your faith and your family will be better for it.

Pray softly...

Lord, give me the strength to say yes to what is really important for my family. Help me to teach them to be more like your servant St. Francis and less like the world.

It's the Most Miserable Time of the Year

Blessed are those who mourn, for they shall be comforted.
—MATTHEW 5:4

Normal Rockwell was a truly gifted twentieth-century artist who was able to capture touching images of American culture, images that were beautiful reflections of average families enjoying life and each other. We see our own perfect families in these lovely paintings, don't we? Don't we wish?

Truth be told, whether it is a Normal Rockwell scene of the family sitting around the dining room table patiently waiting for Dad to carve the turkey or the big brother in the Folger's Coffee commercial who surprises his little sister and parents on Christmas morning, very few of us have picture-perfect families like this—including yours truly. My family is closer to the Cammareri's and the Castorini's of *Moonstruck* fame (only on steroids). We need a Philadelphia lawyer to figure out who is talking to whom, and that's even before we throw the God factor into the mix. "Mama Mia!" as I like to say.

At times family life is anything *but* a pretty picture. In fact, it can be heartbreaking. According to a 2011 report from the Family Research Council only 46 percent of children in the United States will reach the age of seventeen living with their married, biological parents.[7] Another study published by the medical journal *The Lancet* found that children growing up in single parent households are twice as likely as their counterparts to develop serious problems later in life.[8] And this is just one snapshot in terms of today's broken homes. There are countless other problems, such as addictions and abuse, that also factor in. Combine this with the stress of a major holiday, and it's a ticking time bomb. It is not very difficult to see how broken families of all sorts can lead to a family meltdown. No doubt the drama is more prone to occur during the stressful holiday seasons, but the problems don't disappear after you take down and put away the Christmas decorations.

It is important to remember that some family issues may never be solved. In my own situation, although I don't understand it, I have come to accept that certain members of the family just don't want me and my husband in their lives. Despite phone calls, e-mails, and apologies for however I may have offended them, combined with massive amounts of prayer, nothing has changed. Oh, I keep praying for healing. I have put in so many prayer requests at basilicas and shrines around the world, that I'm surprised I haven't received a cease-and-desist notice from the Vatican as the paper trail is getting quite long. Even though I really want God to pull a Loretta Castorini on my estranged relatives and scream, "Snap out of it!" so far that hasn't happened.

I take comfort in the fact that I have tried. I take comfort in the family members with whom I have grown closer because of this particular trial. And I take comfort in an extended family of incredible friends that the Lord has blessed me with since my return to the Church. So Happy Thanksgiving, Buon Natale, Happy New Year, and God bless us everyone.

Pray softly...

Lord, thank you for giving me your Holy Family. Thank you for my extended Christian family to enjoy. I will keep praying for the healing of my own broken relationships.

To Know Him Is to Love Him

If you knew the gift of God and who it is that is saying to you,
"Give me a drink," you would have asked him
and he would have given you living water.

—JOHN 4:10

There is a beautiful quote attributed to the great catechist Fr. John Hardon posted on the bulletin board in my home office. I treasure the quote for two reasons: first because of the words of wisdom and second because of the person who gave me the quote.

I received it from a dear friend, Sr. Joseph Andrew, a renowned catechist in her own right and the cofounder of an amazing religious order, the Sisters of Mary, Mother of the Eucharist. These are the same beautiful sisters featured not once but twice on *Oprah*. Their love of the Lord and life is energizing and captivating to say the least. Sr. Joseph jotted down this Fr. Hardon quote several years ago during an event at which we were both speaking. She gave the quote to me after I shared a bit of my journey back to the Church with her.

There is no power on all the earth as great as a woman when she falls in love with Jesus Christ.

She also told me why it meant so much to her:

Fr. Hardon gave "me" that quote at a very early Mass in 1987 when I was attending the summer school for novice mistresses at Our Lady of Good Council Retreat House in Lincoln, Nebraska. His Mass was really early, and although there were a good number of sisters who were there for the summer, I was the only one that would get up that early and attend Fr. Hardon's Mass. (Then I'd go to the second Mass that all the sisters would attend.) Despite my telling him that he did not need to give me a daily homily since I was the only one in the "congregation," he said, "I give the homily to the universal attendance at Mass…you are just the only one visible to me." And he continued to give me these homilies daily. This one was on the feast of St. Mary Magdalene. Beautiful, isn't it?

It is so beautiful and so true! Let's think about the Samaritan woman who met Jesus at the well (see John 4). This woman came to the well in the middle of the day to avoid being the object of scorn and gossip. After all, she was living with a man who was not her husband and had already had five husbands. She was ashamed, but then she fell in love and everything changed. She didn't know Jesus before that encounter at the well, but after meeting him and having her inner thirst quenched, her life was so dramatically altered that she left her water jug and went into town to tell the people about Jesus—the same people she was hoping to avoid that day. She is considered one of the first evangelists. St. John tells us many people in the town came to believe in Jesus because of her witness.

Why did she fall so head over heels in love with the Lord? Because he loved her where she was at, but he also loved her enough not to leave her there. He told her she deserved better; she was a child of God and worthy of so much more than the life for which she had settled. She didn't feel condemned. She felt loved. And she couldn't help but love in return.

That's what happened to me. Although I had made a mess of my marriage and my life mainly due to my selfish interests, God met me where I was. I can remember one poignant moment during confession shortly after I came back to the Catholic Church. The priest had his eyes closed during our meeting. It was obvious he was not sleeping but really listening as I rolled out a list of venial sins. When I was finished, he opened his eyes and looked straight into my heart. He said nothing about what I had just confessed, but what he did say shook me to the core.

"Why don't you yet see yourself as a loved daughter of the King?"

At that moment I truly appreciated what the Catholic Church teaches about the sacrament of reconciliation: the priest is *in persona*

Christi (in the person of Christ). Jesus was speaking through the priest in that confessional. Although I was back in the Church and trying to put my life back together, I still hadn't quite forgiven myself for all the mistakes I had made. Feeling the love of Christ that day brought me to tears, but it also made me feel like the Samaritan woman—free to go and tell so many others about Jesus.

Pray softly...

Dear Lord, I pray that I will allow myself to meet you at the well in my own life. Please remind me that I am your daughter and that by knowing and loving you, my deepest thirst for true and lasting happiness will be met.

Recipe for Deliverance

Jesus said to her, "Woman, where are they? Has no one condemned you?"
She said, "No one, Lord." And Jesus said, "Neither do I condemn you;
go, and do not sin again."

—John 8:10–11

Each year in suburban Detroit there is a wonderful fashion show entitled "Women Helping Women." It is put on by the Christian ministry Grace Centers of Hope. In addition to professional models, the fashion show features clients who have successfully gone through their faith-based therapy program. Most are dealing with some sort of physical and emotional abuse combined with an alcohol or drug addiction. Some have been put out on the streets with their young children by their husbands or boyfriends. Others were so desperate to feed their families, or perhaps their habit, that they turned to prostitution. For several years I had the blessing of emceeing this event, which often has a butterfly theme. The butterfly represents the women breaking through their former destructive lifestyle and being transformed into a new, beautiful creature in Christ.

That's probably how the adulterous woman felt when she heard the words of Jesus: "Neither do I condemn you; go, and do not sin again."

Jesus wasn't afraid to enter into that very messy situation. While other men stood by ready to stone her to death, Jesus was there two thousand years ago to save her. And he is here today in the twenty-first century to do the same for you and me.

Maybe your past isn't as dramatic as the women gracing the pages of Scripture or walking that fashion runway. But whatever you've done previously, it's time to give it over to God so you can walk with your head held high. Scripture tells us that where sin abounds, grace abounds even more (see Romans 5:20). The world looked at the messy lifestyles of the adulterous woman and the women of Grace Centers and turned its back on them—or worse. The world sees them as recipes for disaster or disasters waiting to happen. Jesus looks at them as a recipe for deliverance. That's how he views us, too. All we need to do is give him a chance.

Pray softly...

Lord, give me the courage to be honest with you about where I'm at these days. I ask you to make me into a new creation, a beautiful example of your grace and mercy.

The Only Thing We Have to Fear Is Those Who Don't Fear Anything

The fear of the Lord is the beginning of wisdom.
—PROVERBS 9:10

Some times when folks hear this proverb, they interpret it to mean that we have to live our lives constantly looking upward or over our shoulder like Chicken Little, running around and worried about the sky falling or the world crumbling beneath our feet the minute we make one big mistake. Or we take this verse to mean that God is a big killjoy who expects us to walk around in sackcloth and ashes and have no fun at all. For some of us, these are the types of messages we received early on in our lives when we were first starting to learn about God—maybe in Catholic grade school or Sunday school. My, how things have changed, though, haven't they? Move forward a few decades and the pendulum has swung completely in the opposite direction.

Don't believe me? Just grab that remote and click on over to your favorite cable channel and check out some of the outlandish reality TV shows. Whether it's *The Real Housewives of New Jersey* or *Keeping Up with the Kardashians,* it's all about living the life of luxury to the point of extreme self-centeredness. The only thing these so called celebs fear is being forced to buy a faux fur.

Now switch over to one of your TV talk shows, news programs, or sports interview channels. You'll see and hear how so many in our society, whether they are politicians, athletes, criminals, or the average person on the street, don't have a fear of much of anything or anyone—certainly not God. We want what we want when we want it, and we want it now regardless of how we go about getting it.

Pope Francis, despite what some in the secular media want you to believe, is not the Pope of the Church of What's Happening Now. His famous "Who am I to judge" statement during that post World Youth Day in-flight press conference[9] was not a clarion call for Catholics and others to make up their own rules regarding core teachings. Nor was he suggesting that we live in a constant state of anxiety, over-burdened by guilt. In a message given during one of his general audiences, he explained how a healthy fear of the Lord should manifest itself in our lives. Pope Francis sees it as a regular internal wake-up call that can lead us to true happiness and fulfillment.

The fear of the Lord is an "alarm." When we are not on the right path, we distance ourselves from God and open ourselves to evil. When we take advantage of others, become attached to money, or succumb to vanity or power or pride, that's when the holy fear of God draws our attention, saying in essence: "You will not be happy like this; this way will end badly." The fear of the Lord is the gift of the Holy Spirit.

It doesn't mean being afraid of God, since we know that God is our Father who always loves and forgives us. It is no servile fear, but rather a joyful awareness of God's grandeur and a grateful realization that only in him do our hearts find true peace. This is the attitude of those who place all their trust in God and feel protected. Through fear of the Lord "we become, as Jesus asks us, like little children, trusting in the goodness and the protection of our heavenly Father."[10]

When you come right down to it, it is those without any moral compass who live without fear of anything or anyone—particularly God, of whom we should be afraid, very afraid.

Pray softly...

Heavenly Father, I pray for all the gifts of your Holy Spirit, but especially today for a healthy fear of the Lord. Thank you that in you alone I can find happiness, freedom, and fulfillment.

Friends in High Places

For I am sure that neither death, nor life, nor angels, nor principalities,
nor the present, nor things to come, nor powers, nor height, nor depth,
nor anything else in all creation, will be able to separate us
from the love of God in Christ Jesus our Lord.
—ROMANS 8:38

"Why do you pray to dead people?" If you're Catholic (or belong to another church that recognizes certain saints), you might have been asked this question before. I know I have. The best response is one given to me by close friend and top Catholic apologist Steve Ray: "Where in the Bible does it say the saints are dead?"

So true! It's so important to remember that we have friends in high places interceding for us. In addition to praying for us in heaven, the lives of the saints are great examples for us—and a powerful source of encouragement.

Let me share one example of one of the powerful experiences I have had with my friends in high places. This encounter with St. Catherine of Siena was particularly meaningful because it occurred during a very stressful week when I was in Rome covering the canonizations of two new saints: John Paul II and John XXIII.

It was April 29, 2014, and I was wrapping up my coverage of the canonizations as well as cohosting a pilgrimage and doing my radio show live from the Eternal City. And then there was the jet lag. April 29 happens to be St. Catherine's feast day. I love St. Catherine because she respectfully but oh so strongly challenged the religious leaders of her day to do the right thing. She didn't mince words and always pointed the way to Christ. The fourteenth century was a very challenging time for the Catholic Church and the papacy. It was Catherine who pointed the pope back to Rome from Avignon, France, and he followed her advice.

The tomb of St. Catherine is located in the Church of Santa Maria sopra Minerva in Rome, tucked behind the Pantheon. On April 29, her tomb (located under the high altar) is actually opened. Visitors can go inside, say a prayer, and actually touch the tomb of this much-loved and admired saint. I had done this only once before in my many trips to Rome, and since this particular trip allowed me to be there again on her feast day, I was determined to get back to the church for some quality time with Caterina.

Well, wouldn't you know it—the day got away from me. In addition to my radio show and some TV spots I was doing for EWTN (Eternal Word TV Network), I was also busy recording other interviews and being interviewed myself. Getting to the church to pray and pay my regards to St. Catherine wasn't going to happen. My personal pity party began.

It was almost 5:00 p.m. I had to rush over to St. Peter's Square to be interviewed by the NBC affiliate in Detroit for a documentary on women in the Church. After our initial greeting, we began to walk away from the square and down the main avenue leading toward the Tiber River. The camera crew had moved to another area a few blocks from the basilica in order to have some different scenery for our segment. To say I was speechless when we arrived at our destination is an understatement.

At our location along the Tiber and next to the Castel Sant'Angelo is a stunning and quite large marble statue of the great saint. For whatever reason, I had forgotten about the statue as we were walking. We ended up recording my TV interview directly across from this magnificent sculpture. I was actually facing St. Catherine the entire time I was on camera. This particular statue is one of those pieces of art that takes your breath away because it is so lifelike. She is featured in flowing robes and appears to be moving or leaning right toward you with a look of intense love, concern, and compassion on her delicate face. During the interview I felt as if she was looking right at me and saying, "No worries, girlfriend, I've got your back. I'm here for you, visit or no visit to my tomb. Carry on, little sister."

Coincidence? Hardly. How about a "God-cidence"? Rome is a huge city, and the area surrounding the Vatican offers countless photo ops, as you might imagine. So why *that* location on *that* day? I think you know the answer.

Whatever your church or denomination, or even if you're still trying to figure out where you belong, don't hesitate to read, learn, and call upon the saints. Remember that you really do have friends in high places who like pointing you in the right direction.

Pray softly...

Thank you, Lord, for the communion of saints—the great cloud of witnesses that intercede for us in heaven around your throne. Please help me to remember to ask for their help and intercession, especially in my efforts to know and love you more deeply.

Don't Ask What God Can Do for You—Ask What You Can Do for God

Seek first his kingdom and his righteousness,
and all these things shall be yours as well.
—MATTHEW 6:33

I was mad at God. Of course, at that time in my life I had little or no relationship with God, but I sure was mad at him. I found it quite easy and convenient to blame him for my troubles.

"If God really loved me, why would he allow this to happen?"

That's what I asked my husband, Dominick, after a painful job loss. About a year before I was fired from a prominent TV position, Dominick had experienced a reversion to our Catholic faith. He was on fire for Christ and the Church and had been encouraging me to take my faith seriously. But my life had been going just fine, thank you. I had achieved a great deal of success in broadcast news fairly quickly. I was at the top of my game, and I had gotten there by achieving one career goal after another all by my lonesome (or so I thought) through lots of hard work, including too many holidays and weekends to count. I had sacrificed a lot to "make it." And then suddenly my lucrative TV contract wasn't renewed, and my world was shattered. Now what?

The problem was, it was the world according to "me, myself, and I." Even though I was raised Catholic and considered myself to be a Christian, I gave barely a moment's notice to what God's will for my life might be. Being fired from my job became one of the biggest blessings of my life, even though I didn't realize it at the time. That experience eventually led me back to Jesus and the Church.

In a daily homily Pope Francis discussed the importance of allowing God to disrupt our plans referring to the Old Testament reading of Jonah and the whale. You're probably familiar with how Jonah got a message from God to go to Nineveh. He ignored the message. He attempted to chart his own course. But instead Jonah was tossed into the sea, swallowed by a whale, and ended up in Nineveh after the whale spit him out onto the seashore.

Jonah, Pope Francis said, had his own life in order: he served the Lord and perhaps he even prayed a great deal. But he didn't want God to disturb his way of life; he didn't want God to interfere with his choices. He tried to escape God's voice. He wanted to write his own story.

The pope said that we can be a lot like that, too. "I say to myself, and I say to you: do we let God write our lives? Or do we want to do the writing ourselves?" Pope Francis asked, according to Vatican Radio.[11]

Learning how to seek God first led to a new and much more fulfilling life for me. God surprised me, and he will surprise you, too, if you let him.

Pray softly...

Lord, please help me to understand that everything begins and ends with you. Help me to start each day by putting my life in your hands. Guide me as I seek to discover and fulfill your special will for my life instead of my own.

They Fought the Lord and the Lord Won

He fell to the ground and heard a voice saying to him
"Saul, Saul, why do you persecute me?"
—ACTS 9:4

You just have to love St. Paul and St. Augustine, not only for their mega contributions to Christianity but also because in so many ways they're a lot like any one of us who has ever tried to run away as fast as she could from Jesus. In Paul's case, initially he not only rejected Christ, he hunted down the Lord's followers and threw many of them in jail (or worse). Augustine hopped on a ship at one point and figured taking to the high seas was the best way to run from God and the prayers of his mom, St. Monica. Nice try.

Eventually the Apostle Paul and Church Father Augustine cried "Uncle!" and said in effect, "We give up, Lord—you win." Since these two men are such Christian rock stars, you might be familiar with their testimonies. But I never get tired of hearing how they came to know Christ. Their journeys provide a lot of food for thought and reflection.

St. Paul, formerly known as Saul of Tarsus before converting to Christianity, was an extremely learned Jew who went around persecuting those who believed in Jesus. He described himself as being advanced in Judaism beyond many of his peers, and he truly believed he was doing right by God in rounding up and severely persecuting Jesus's followers. He is considered an apostle, although not one of the twelve as he didn't meet Jesus until after the Lord's resurrection on the road to Damascus. He was knocked off his high horse both figuratively and literally, and blinded for three days. Then, when he regained his sight, he saw things much differently. Paul went from being one of Christianity's toughest critics to one of its most fervent promoters. He is considered one of the greatest writers of the New Testament; fourteen of the twenty-seven books of the New Testament are attributed to him. He spent his last days in Rome, and although his death is not recorded in Scripture, it is believed that he was martyred there.

St. Augustine of Hippo was born of a Christian mother and a pagan father. But it didn't take long for Augustine to show that he had no interest in Christianity. He was an intellectual, so he was able to do well in his studies while getting into all kinds of other trouble at the same time. He lived with a woman, had a child out of wedlock, and dabbled in all sorts of different religions in his search for the truth. Years later he moved to Milan. Then, after having his own conversion experience and spending time with the bishop there (St. Ambrose), Augustine's life, like St. Paul's, did a 180. In addition to his famous *Confessions*, he left behind a huge body of sermons and other works and is a doctor of the Catholic Church.

Both St. Paul and St. Augustine were in a real tug of war with the Lord. But then Jesus grabbed their hearts. For St. Paul, it happened in an instant. St. Augustine's journey was a longer one. But if the Lord can change the hearts of these two brilliant and quite stubborn men, he can change anybody. Never forget that every saint has a past and every sinner has a future.

Pray softly...

Lord, you win. I have been fighting with you long enough. I may never be a St. Paul or a St. Augustine, but I place my life in your hands.

Don't Cry Over Spilled Perfume

She is clothed with strength and dignity;
she can laugh at the days to come.
—Proverbs 31:25

We've all had those days, probably too many to count, where having a good laugh is about the last thing on our minds. You know, the days when you just can't seem to get it together. Or you think you have it together when you walk out the door, only to realize when you get to where you are going you are wearing the wrong colored shoes, have a very long run in your stockings plus a coffee stain on your blouse you didn't notice when you looked in the mirror.

These are minor inconveniences in the bigger scheme of things. Why do these little spills of life seem to usually happen before an important meeting at work or a social event we were really looking forward to? How about flying halfway across the country for a major presentation and arriving without your luggage—including, heaven forbid, your cosmetic bag? That happened to me a few years ago the night before a major women's conference.

If we're not careful, these minor inconveniences can really throw us off our spiritual game. We all want to accomplish the tasks of the day with confidence and a sense of pride. It's understandable that, when these types of annoyances happen, our anxiety goes up and our confidence makes a beeline for the down elevator. In my case, I made a dash for the nearest CVS, grabbed some makeup essentials, and made the best of it by wearing the same business suit for my seminar that I had worn on the plane. The show must go on, and so did I. My suitcase arrived the next day (after my presentation, of course). But no one was the wiser, and I was the only one who could tell the difference between the Cover Girl and the Clinique.

This is exactly the time to make a choice. We can either let wardrobe malfunctions dominate the moment, or we can rise above the bad shoe selection, have a good laugh about it, and forge ahead. The less you make of it, the less anyone will notice, and the less your peace of mind and spirit will be impacted. Never let those around you—in particular, the devil—see you sweat.

Pray softly...

Heavenly Father, remind me that because I am your child I am always clothed in dignity and strength. I can laugh at any wardrobe malfunction or other mishap that may come along as long as I keep my eyes focused on you.

Mirror, Mirror on the Wall, Who's the Fattest of Them All?

I praise you, for I am wondrously made.
Wonderful are your works! You know me right well.
—Psalm 139:14

"Wondrously made? Yeah, right! Not me." Yes, *you*—yes, all of us, even though quite often we don't feel that way because we are too busy comparing ourselves to someone else when we look in the mirror. Maybe it is a friend who never struggled with her weight and looks the same in her forties as she did in college. Or the mom down the street— you know, the one with several children, who never has a hair out of place and who can still fit into her leggings without two pairs of Spanx? And this comparison is just for starters. Just to make sure we are the most pathetic looking women on planet Earth, we continue the "I'm uglier than Medusa" routine by thumbing through the latest edition or *InStyle* or *People*. To add even more insult to injury, we then turn on the TV and start judging our appearance against runway models and Hollywood starlets, women who have makeup artists, plastic surgeons, personal chefs, and personal trainers at their beck and call 24/7. We are regularly sending ourselves negative messages about our appearance—particularly our size, even though the average woman in America is a size twelve or fourteen.

A recent *Glamour* magazine survey found that, on average, women have about thirteen negative body thoughts per day. (That's nearly one for every waking hour.) Glamour also reported that "a disturbing number of women confess to having 35, 50, or even 100 hateful thoughts about their own shapes each day."[12]

So what were the more than three hundred women surveyed by *Glamour* actually saying to themselves about their body size or appearance?

"You are a fat, worthless pig."

"No man is ever going to want you."

"Ugly. Big. Gross."[13]

In many ways this is not at all surprising when we considered our media-saturated culture. Even the most faithful among us struggle with this and probably will for most of our lives. We're human, and we are surrounded by a constant bombardment of messages trying to convince us that we are only good enough if we can fit into J Crew's 000 jeans or pull a Bethenny Frankel and proudly pose—as the former reality TV star did in the summer of 2014—in her four-year-old daughter's pajamas![14]

So stop comparing yourself to ridiculously unrealistic media images and women who are just out for attention, do not represent the majority of us, and (if the truth be known) are really hankering for a big fat cheeseburger or a salami sandwich. Things are hardly as they seem. When it comes to advertising, remember these two very important terms: *airbrushing* and *digital alterations*. According to one report, women spend an average of $15,000 dollars on cosmetics in their lifetime; $20 billion is spent each year in this country on dieting products.[15] Any doubt that technology is used and misused to increase supply and demand particularly in the cosmetic, clothing, and weight-loss industries? Yet so many educated women, myself included, are still influenced by the images they see in the media.

If the Creator of the universe thinks we are wondrously made, who are we to think otherwise?

Pray softly...

Jesus, please help me see myself as you see me and not as I often see myself. Give me the strength to stop comparing myself to false and unhealthy images in the media and make the most of the wonderful body you have given me.

Necessity Is the Mother of the Microwave

Do your best to present yourself to God as one approved,
a worker who has no need to be ashamed,
rightly handling the word of truth.
—2 TIMOTHY 2:15

In a perfect world it sure would be nice to be able to prepare—or come home to—a spotless house and a homemade meal every night. Last time I checked, however, we don't live in a perfect world. Scripture tells us we live in a fallen world due to original sin. It is also a fast-paced one with plenty of two-income or single-parent households—families who are trying to do their best and juggle busy schedules with work, school, home, and after-school activities.

Slowing down enough to make room for the Lord in your life includes not putting so much pressure on yourself to expect perfection all the time on the home front. We women, after all, tend to have degrees in guilt. I'm Italian and Catholic, so I have advanced degrees in this category. But what's more important—spending time with God and your family or making ravioli from scratch? (Notice I didn't say making the sauce from scratch, because in my family not doing so is grounds for being cut out of the will, disowned, or worse.)

Let me share a real-life story from one of the more reasonable members of my Italian American brood in hopes that it will give you a little more reassurance the next time you start to feel like you're the worst parent or wife in the world for ordering takeout or heating up some soup in the microwave for dinner.

When my cousin Jean's children were still in Catholic grade school, she found herself in a bit of a domestic pickle. Each year before Christmas break, the school would have a party and students would volunteer to bring a treat. Well, that year Jean's youngest son, Danny, volunteered Mom to bake something for the festivities. Come the morning of the event, as Jean was running around grabbing lunches, backpacks, and the like, Danny wondered out loud where she was hiding the homemade treats. Suddenly Jean realized she had totally forgotten about her commitment. She ran to the pantry, pretending she had everything under control. Lo and behold, she found a box of Little Debbie Swiss Rolls. She also remembered she had some green decorative icing and red candies—baking supplies she was going to use when she finally got around to baking those Christmas cookies. She grabbed all three items, and after a few drops of that green icing and a few of those cute little red candies, by golly, those Swiss Rolls turned into lovely Christmas Yule logs! They were the hit of the party, and no one was the wiser. My cousin didn't forget about the dessert because she was a careless mom. She just had been busy doing more important activities with her children.

So the bottom line here is to stop treating guilt as the gift that keeps on giving. Simply do the best you can by the Lord and your family. And remember, as humorist Erma Bombeck once said, "No one ever died from sleeping in an unmade bed."[16] I think you get the picture.

Pray softly...

Lord, you know my heart. You know my daily struggles and challenges as I try to do my best for you and my family. Help me to remember that you don't expect me to be perfect—just faithful.

Walk a Mile in Her Jimmy Choos

Bear one another's burdens, and so fulfil the law of Christ.
—GALATIANS 6:2

Years ago when my husband and I were scheduled to give our marriage testimony at a huge function in Detroit, I panicked. Although we had been back in the Church for almost ten years at that point, I was still a public person. I was no longer working in the secular media; I now hosted a talk show on Christian radio. There were over five hundred people in attendance at this couples' dinner, and I just didn't think I could go through with putting that much of my private life out there for the entire world—at least my portion of the world—to see. Of course, it didn't help matters any that I had just gotten off the phone with a friend of mine, another media personality, who pretty much convinced me that sharing my journey back to wholeness would destroy my image and eventually my career.

So we called a close friend of ours, Deacon Bob Ovies of the Archdiocese of Detroit. After explaining my concern, he said something that sticks with me to this day: "Teresa, everybody's got something. Do you actually think you and Dom are the only couple to ever struggle and come close to divorce? Who knows how many people you two will help by just telling it like it is!"

We decided to go through with the talk. It wasn't easy, but Deacon Bob was spot on. Afterward, so many couples came forward and shared that they, too, had walked a similar path. To hear it from someone else gave them the courage to work on their own marriages.

That was more than fifteen years ago. My husband and I have shared our marriage testimony many times since then, and each time we do, the same thing happens. It's not that we're such dazzling speakers. It's the simple fact that when we take the time to tell others that we have made mistakes but there is hope in Jesus, people respond. Often we miss opportunities to carry each other's burdens because we think their world is perfect and they couldn't possibly have any problems. Or we assume something about someone else based on appearances, not really knowing what is going on in their lives. We may think badly of them or even struggle with feelings of jealousy based on what we believe to be true, which in reality is most likely far from the truth.

So whether they're Jimmy Choos, Pradas, or Payless, walking in our sisters' shoes can make this journey through life much more rewarding.

Pray softly...

Dear Lord, help me to encourage others reminding them that they are not alone in their pain. Remind me to reach out to others by remembering we all have something and we all need to help carry each other's burdens.

Bling It On!

Again, the kingdom of heaven is like a merchant in search of fine pearls,
who, on finding one pearl of great value, went and sold
all that he had and bought it.
—MATTHEW 13:45–46

What girl doesn't like at least a little bling? Even if you're not one to accessorize daily, you probably have one or two pieces of jewelry that you really love and just can't live without. Then there are those of us who can set our hearts on a piece of jewelry that is much bigger than our wallets. We buy it anyway because we just *have* to have it. Still others insist on wearing that necklace or pair of earrings they adore, even though it's just not a good look for them.

That's why I love the story *The Pearl Necklace*. It's all about the bling thing—faux verses real bling, in the spiritual sense. Jenny, the story's main character, is a lot like most of us. We set our sights on something we want, and once we get it we don't want to let go, even if the bling to which we're clinging is tarnishing before our very eyes and turning our neck, wrists, or perhaps our lives green.

For weeks and weeks, Jenny had her mind set on a set of faux pearls she spotted in the dime store. Finally she saved up two dollars, just enough to buy them, and she was thrilled. She wore her purchase everywhere and took the necklace off only to take a bath. She even wore her pearls to bed. That necklace made her feel like a princess. Meanwhile, while Jenny was enjoying her pearls, she was having a hard time understanding why her Daddy kept insisting that she give him her prized necklace. He knew how she saved every penny to buy them on her own, but each night after reading her a bedtime story, he would ask her to hand over the pearls. She kept saying no and instead would offer him her favorite doll or stuffed animal, which he refused to accept. For some reason he wanted those faux pearls.

Finally one night it dawned on Jenny that since her father loved her so much, there must be a good reason why he was so persistent in pursuing her prized pearls. So, with tears in her eyes, she handed over her faux pearls. In return he reached into his pocket and gave her a strand of precious real pearls in exchange. He had the real pearls all the time. He was just waiting for her to hand over the fake necklace so he could give her a strand of precious, priceless, real pearls.

What is the faux pearl necklace in your life? Are you willing to turn over the cheap strand of pearls in exchange for God's special plan for you? I know it's scary to let go of our own agenda. Jenny, however, was confident enough in her father's love to trust that he wouldn't let her down. Are you?

Pray softly...

Lord, I want real and lasting happiness, not the dime-store version of fulfillment. Please show me how my own stubbornness maybe blocking your precious plan for my life. Help me discover the pearl of great price through a deeper relationship with you.

You Are What You Tweet

I am saying this for your own benefit, not to lay any restraint upon you,
but to promote good order and to secure you undivided devotion to the Lord.
—1 Corinthians 7:35

I like to think of the word BIBLE as an acronym: Basic Instructions Before Leaving Earth. I mean, how much clearer could Scripture be regarding the need to focus when it comes to our faith than this sobering verse from St. Paul in 1 Corinthians? How many of us ever stop to think about how distracted we really are? Take media usage, for example. I travel regularly and love to people-watch at the airports. It's interesting to see just how many devices people not only carry with them but use at one time. These days it's not uncommon to see someone talking on a cell phone, tapping away on an iPad, all while sitting in front of a TV screen in the airport lounge or restaurant. Mamma Mia! Or TMI: too much information!

When I give media-awareness presentations, most adults are stunned to learn that the average American spends almost as much time on the job every day as they do tweeting, posting, e-mailing, and surfing the Web—more than five hours a day, according to a number of reports.[17] And this statistic does not include television-viewing time. The parents in my audiences are even more horrified to learn that American children on average consume fifty-three hours of media per week. Add to that the other activities that fill our waking hours at home or in the office or both; is it any wonder we don't hear from God or can't seem to figure out God's will for our life? The time factor alone is frightening, not to mention the content or lack thereof found in today's media outlets, whatever form.

No one is suggesting that you toss that smartphone and laptop into the garbage. These devices are helpful and, in many ways, necessary forms of communication. They're a must in the business world and have also become incredible tools for evangelization. Pope Francis has a huge following on Twitter, and recently the Vatican has put forth a new effort to improve its social media outreach. Christians in general find the Internet to be a very successful alternative way to promote religious events and have become experts at it. In addition the Internet serves society well when it comes to aiding law enforcement on a variety of levels or even addressing a community crisis such as when a natural disaster occurs.

But let's be honest here. While I would like to think that most people are using these devices for more noble causes, this is simply not the case. Most of the time it's idle chatter, playing games, and unfortunately all to often engaging in immoral behavior, including accessing pornography—activities that can greatly impact our relationship with God through temptation and sin.

So do yourself a favor and conduct a media reality check. Take an honest look at your media usage. Think about practical ways you can cut back and still be able to function in your day-to-day responsibilities. Let that cell phone downtime be your time with God.

Pray softly...

Dear Lord, show me how my media usage may be negatively affecting the most important relationships in my life, starting with my relationship with you. As challenging as it may be, help me see how my time on the Internet or in front of the TV might influence my behavior and thinking in negative ways. Strengthen me in my efforts to curb bad media habits.

Blood, Sweat, and Years

Do not be weary in well-doing.
—2 THESSALONIANS 3:13

"How long did it take you to heal your marriage? How long before you figured out God's plan for your life? How long?" These are questions I hear often. The answers didn't happen in a matter of a few weeks or a few months. In both my personal and professional life, it took years to get them back on track. Even now, life doesn't run smoothly all the time and often veers off course. But through perseverance, determination, and most importantly through the love and grace of God, the ride has become a lot easier and much more pleasant to navigate.

Unfortunately, many are extremely disappointed with my response. We live in a microwave, fast-food, express-lane society. We are used to getting answers instantaneously and getting what we want quickly, very quickly.

On some levels most of us realize certain things don't happen at the snap of our fingers. For example, someone studying to be a doctor is willing to put in the years of schooling and hundreds of thousands of dollars in training and education that it takes to eventually get that medical license. If we are concerned about staying healthy we put in more than thirty minutes a week at the gym. We are willing to put in long hours on the job and take some additional classes in order to get that promotion or corner office. We accept the media messages as truth when it comes to working hard to get ahead and stay in shape.

The media gives us the opposite impressions when it comes to matters of faith and family, however—messages we have also accepted wholeheartedly, but to our detriment. We see couples and their wedding parties poring over china patterns, bridal magazines, and reception menus. That looks like fun. Everybody into the pool! But in real life, as opposed to reality TV (which is anything but real life), talk to your local priest or minister, and they will paint quite a different scenario. You'll hear tale after tale of unhappy brides and grooms balking at spending more than a weekend or an evening in marriage prep. Well, of course they want to get married in a church. But what does God have to do with it? The church instead has become a nice backdrop for wedding photos. And we wonder why half of all marriages in this country, including Christian marriages, still end in divorce.

Regarding our relationship with God, the same approach applies. We walk away from God or find a comfortable religion that doesn't require us to go very deep. We want the Ten Suggestions, not the Ten Commandments. This way we can do what we want and fool ourselves into thinking we have God's approval.

Not so, said the great writer, poet, and theologian G.K. Chesterton: "The Christian ideal has not been tried and found wanting. It has been found difficult; and left untried."[18]

Pray softly...

Lord, please forgive me for putting so much effort into other areas of my life and yet taking our relationship so lightly. I will work harder at putting you first in hope of getting my life in order, no matter how long it takes.

All Sunshine Makes a Desert— and Very Dry Skin

We know that in everything God works for good
with those who love him,
who are called according to his purpose.
—Romans 8:28

A few years after I came back to the Catholic Church, I enrolled in a Bible study class. It consisted of weekly gatherings where we broke into small groups and went over the questions related to the assigned Scriptural passages. The discussions were followed by a thirty-minute lecture from the group leader. I will never forget, having just gone through some trying personal and professional challenges of my own, how our group leader's message one week really struck home. We had been reviewing some verses in the New Testament on suffering. The lesson was designed to help us understand how suffering can produce great fruit in our lives. We discussed how, if we allow God to work through them, sufferings can make us stronger, give us a greater appreciation for the blessings in our lives, and bring us closer to Christ. Our Bible study leader used what she referred to as an old Arab proverb to drive home the point that it is the tough times, not the days and nights on easy street, that can mold us and make us into the best we can be. "All sunshine makes a desert," she said. (Or, as I like to say, "a desert—and very dry skin.")

I could relate to the sunshine part so very easily. I live in Michigan, which does not exactly consist of sunny, balmy weather all year round. And yet, wouldn't you know it, summer is my favorite time of year. However, would I appreciate the glorious Michigan summers along the Great Lakes if we had sunshine seven days a week year round? And given that catching some rays happens to be another favorite thing of mine, what would my skin look like if I spent too much time in the sun? Most likely instead of a healthy bronze glow, my face might more closely resemble a pitted prune. And in terms of my life experiences, instead of a healthy appreciation for how close I came to losing what matters most, my world might be a very dry and empty place.

I don't know anyone who *enjoys* suffering. Most of us head into the latest trial or struggle with much trepidation and fear, not to mention a good dose of kicking and screaming. Will we be OK? Will our family or our jobs be secure? How will our lives look once we come out on the other side? And yet, when I stop to take a deep breath and remember how good the Lord has been, I have to admit that although I may not want to experience a particular trial ever again, it is that very trial that brought me much further along in my faith—making me realize that the change of seasons, even the coldest of winters, are necessary for a new springtime and eventually that sunny summer place.

Pray softly...

Sweet Jesus, I sometimes forget that we live in a fallen world and that nothing will be perfect until, God willing, we meet you face-to-face in heaven. When I get frustrated with the storms of life, please show me again how you not only always calm the storm but bring me through it safely.

When Life Gives You Lemons, Make Limoncello!

Count it all joy, my brothers and sisters, whenever you face trials of many kinds, because the testing of your faith produces perseverance.
—James 1:2–3, *NIV*

Ah, Limoncello, the delectable after-dinner drink of the famous Amalfi Coast along Italy's southern Mediterranean shores. Served ice cold, and usually after meals in the hot summer months, a few sips of this lovely liquor and you feel like you are Queen or *Principessa* for a day. It is easy to imagine yourself sunbathing on the serene Isle of Capri or strolling the magical streets of Sorrento. Limoncello is very strong, very smooth, and very good. It is also quite a process to get the fine finished product poured ever so carefully into beautiful bottles delicately and colorfully painted with scenes of the stunning coastline from where it originates. On my many trips to Italy, I have encountered a number of different native Italians, from tour guides to hotel operators, whose family has their own Limoncello recipe. That family recipe is a treasured part of their heritage. While the time and effort that goes into making this drink is very involved, the end result is worth it.

Wind the clock back a few weeks or months, and see exactly what it takes to make Limoncello. No pun intended, but as my Grandma

Anna Tomeo used to say, "It's not all peaches and cream, you know." No, it's actually the skins from a certain type of lemon that are peeled and soaked and thrown into a mixture of grain alcohol and sugar water. The liquid is heated on the stove for some time and then left to soak for weeks at a time until it's after-dinner debut. Just like with lemonade, the lemons don't just pop off the trees and into the pitcher. They have to be pulled from the tree, sliced, squeezed, mixed, and sometimes processed (depending on whether we're talking fresh or store-bought). In other words, making Limoncello or lemonade is a process—and for the lemons, it's a painful one. But when Italian families sit down around the family table, especially the families who make their own lemon concoction, they don't gulp it down. They savor every drop as they recall the effort that was put into turning the lemons into Limoncello.

Life can be a lot like Limoncello. If we want to make something of ourselves and make our mark in this life for the Lord, it usually comes after a lot of pruning, peeling, processing, and soaking. God prunes those he loves. Just as the lemon trees along the Amalfi Coast are pruned to grow the perfect lemons, God prunes us to ensure that we, too, will bear fruit. We go through our own peeling, processing, and soaking. A lemon eaten by itself can be very sour. And just like the sufferings and growth process, it isn't exactly pleasant to experience. But the steps we take to enter into a relationship with the Lord also don't come by just hanging around on some branches or at our local parish all day long. We have to allow our good qualities to get steeped in God's Word. We have to work on our prayer life, learn to forgive, and continually turn everything over to God. In other words, we have to endure some level of discomfort or suffering in order to get to the good stuff in the pretty bottles. Once we crack open the long-awaited treat, just like a better life in Christ, it is to be savored and greatly appreciated.

Pray softly...

Dear Lord, please help me understand how suffering can bring great fruit in my life if I allow myself to learn from the experience. In the midst of my struggles, let me bask in the warmth of your Son and know that when I come through the fermenting process I will have grown stronger, and wiser, and closer to you.

Misery or Ministry?

And after you have suffered a little while, the God of all grace,
who has called you to his eternal glory in Christ,
will himself restore, establish, and strengthen you.
—1 Peter 5:10

At some point, if we hang in there with God, we'll understand that if he brings us to it, he will see us through it. However, the Lord might want to use this suffering for more than just a one-time lesson in patience and endurance.

In my case, my misery turned into a full-time ministry. Many of the things I experienced, including challenges in my relationship with God and my husband as well professional challenges and a whole lot of dumb mistakes on my part, have made for a lifetime's worth of speaking, writing, and radio material. (As I said in the introduction, I am a major work in progress.)

Think about some of the charities, ministries, and activists groups that have been born out of great loss and suffering. Candy Lightner started the movement Mothers against Drunk Driving after her daughter Cari was killed by a drunk driver. John Walsh cofounded the National Center for Missing and Exploited Children after his son

Adam was abducted and killed. Before Lightner's efforts, drunk driving was not taken seriously. Since MADD began, more than four hundred laws have been enacted and public attitude toward the problem has dramatically changed. John Walsh's work has become internationally known and led to the passage of the Missing Children Act of 1982.

Your situation might not be as traumatic as the Candy's and John's, but God might be trying to show you that, in addition to your own spiritual growth, your suffering could be put to use in other ways. And the pain you're experiencing now might not warrant a full-time commitment. You're probably in much better psychological shape than yours truly, but it is certainly worth praying about.

Pray softly...

Lord, is there a bigger lesson here that you're trying to teach me? If there is, Lord, your will be done. Just show me how you want me to use my misery to minister somehow to others.

Jesus: The Real Quicker Picker Upper

As far as the east is from the west,
so far does he remove our transgressions from us.
—Psalm 103:12

Let's go back a few years to TV archive land and revisit an adorable commercial selling Bounty paper towels. The commercial shows a sweet little boy dressed in a cowboy outfit. You can tell just by the look on his face that he thinks he is one cool dude. He comes barreling into the kitchen, boots, spurs, and all. With great gusto he reaches up to the counter and grabs a pitcher of juice on the counter. Suddenly the pitcher tips over and spills all over the floor. He starts to cry, and Mom, looking at her baby boy with forgiving eyes, grabs a few paper towels and makes the sticky mess go away as if it never happened. As we are watching this touching scene, we hear the announcer say: "When spills are at their worst, Bounty is at its best."

Sounds a lot like the Lord, doesn't it? Often we are not that much different than that little boy in the Bounty commercial. We think we're all dressed up and raring to go, ready to take on life. Then we are sidetracked by a mistake—something a lot bigger than spilled juice. We feel guilty. We feel ashamed, and depending on the level of sin, our indiscretions, like the little cowboy in the Bounty ad, may cause us to want to run, hide, and cry. If we turn to God, however, we will find that he reacts in the same way as the loving mom does. God doesn't look at us with condemnation or scorn, but with forgiveness, love, and mercy. He has roll after roll of paper towels that can wipe our slate clean, not just once, but repeatedly.

God's forgiveness can seem too good to be true. That's because we look at it in human terms. OK, we get that a good mother is not going to issue a ten-hour time-out for some routine spills. But God is God, and sin just can't be cleaned up that quickly—or so we think. This is not to say there aren't consequences to sin. There definitely are. God knows our hearts, and he knows if we are simply trying to abuse his gift of mercy by claiming we can do whatever we want because he is going to forgive us any way. That said, Scripture tells us if we are truly sorry, forgiveness and mercy are new every morning (see Lamentations 3:23).

Just what a cowboy or cowgirl needs to get back in the saddle of life again.

Pray softly...

Dear Lord, sometimes your forgiveness seems too good to be true. I'm a lot like that little boy in the Bounty commercial—so raring to go and at the same time such a klutz. Please help me see that, no matter how messy my mistakes are or how many I make, as long as I have a sincere heart, you are ready to give me another chance.

Time for a Faith Lift

Be strong, and let your heart take courage,
all you who wait for the Lord!
—PSALM 31:24

Because I am in ministry full-time and because I am definitely an extrovert, people sometimes assume that I am always in a great mood, always ready to go and conquer the world for Christ. No doubt I love what I do, but what I do can also be challenging. When I look out at all that is wrong with the world and see so many attacks against Christians, feelings of frustration and despair can take over. Being in ministry, I naturally hear and see a lot of what's wrong with the world firsthand.

The climate around Catholics and other Christians has been growing increasingly hostile over the last few years. Religious groups, family-owned businesses, and Catholic dioceses have been forced to go to court to protect their religious freedoms. Private citizens have been practically tarred and feathered in the public square for donating to efforts to protect the institution of marriage between a man and a woman—an institution that has been the bedrock of society for thousands of years. Christian martyrdom is becoming all too common in certain parts of the world, particularly in Iraq and other parts of the troubled Middle East. Therefore, every once in a while the bad news gets to me. The good news is that God continually reminds me that he is very large and still very much in charge.

In July 2014 I headed to Philadelphia to cover a Catholic conference; this was during a very tumultuous time following the Supreme Court decision dealing with religious liberty. The ruling was a victory for Christians. However the vitriol from those who disagreed was over the top and a horrible misinformation campaign from the same camp was relentless. My heart was heavy as I got to the event. When I arrived, however, I seemed to be the only one down in the dumps. It's not as if those attending were pretending that everything was just fine and dandy. They just knew they had the answer to the world's problems—the truth, as in The Truth: Jesus Christ. I was overwhelmed by their joy and enthusiasm, and I was so encouraged by the number of young people involved in various Catholic ministries who obviously were busy preaching in and out of season. This particular conference had more than doubled its attendance since the same gathering two years earlier. I knew the Lord was telling me, "Chill out, my daughter, and just keep doing what you're doing."

Nothing like a day at the spiritual spa, including a faith lift!

Pray softly...

Dear Lord, please remind me that it is not my responsibility to try and fix all the problems in the world or to carry the weight of the world on my shoulders. Encourage me to keep preaching in and out of season and to remember that you really do have the entire universe in your hands.

God's "Yes"

If you keep my commandments, you will abide in my love, just as I have kept my Father's commandments and abide in his love.

—JOHN 15:10

Following the election of Pope Francis in March of 2013, Catholic commentator and bestselling author George Weigel spent a lot of time with reporters discussing the former Cardinal Bergoglio from Argentina, as well as the future of the Church.

The interviewers did their best to haul out topics they considered highly suspect: traditional marriage, contraception, the male priesthood, and so on. I know George well and have had the privilege of interviewing him on my own program. To say that I have respect for him is a huge understatement. Despite the obvious ignorance of journalists regarding so many things Catholic, George not only keeps his cool but really knows how to drive home key points. He may not change the reporter's mind, but if viewers are paying attention, George will cause them to think twice about what the Church teaches.

During one particular network interview, George gave what I consider to be a show-stopper of an answer after the anchor went on and on about how the Church needed to conform to the world instead of the other way around. "When the Church says no, it's because no leads to an elevated 'yes,'" he said.[19]

If you're a mom, you probably get what George Weigel is saying. Little Sammy may think that riding his new bike in the middle of a busy street looks like fun, weaving in and out of moving vehicles and playing his own version of Dodge 'Em. Your answer is of course going to be a big, fat *no*. Why? Because you realize as Sammy's parent, your "no" could literally save his life. In other words, it's a "yes."

It's funny how we totally get it when it comes to saying no to children. But when it comes to God saying no to us regarding hot button, below-the-belt issues, we turn around and act like children ourselves. Observing some of the recent reaction to the Church staying true to its teachings, we look like those kids at the toy store who drop to the floor kicking and screaming when Mommy or Daddy refuses to give them every last item on the shelves. Maybe God says no to us, as Benedict XVI told a group of young people in Italy a few years ago, for the same reasons: because he made us, he loves us, and he knows what will truly make us happy—which does not translate into doing whatever we want with whomever we want.

God wants to give us a great big "yes" that leads to life and love.

Pray softly...

Dear Lord, I admit there are times I struggle with some of your commandments. Please give me the strength to go deeper and really understand why you, as my Father, know what's best for me and my long-term joy and fulfillment.

Fifty Shades of Grace

Where sin increased, grace abounded all the more.
—Romans 5:20

I was in grade school when the so-called women's liberation movement really started to take hold. I remember seeing lots of stories and newspaper headlines about women taking to the streets, demanding equal pay, better job opportunities, and better treatment all around. One very strong message of that era had to do with not being treated as an object—a sexual object in particular.

Fast-forward nearly five decades later: As what women once protested so loudly has now become a societal norm, we can see how, in the area of sexuality, the feminist movement made a major turn in the wrong direction. If this is feminism, I'm out of here—exit stage left. Where are these "feminists" now? How did we go from demanding we be recognized for our brains and not just our bra size to the likes of Anastasia Steele in the novel *Fifty Shades of Grey*? How in the world did bondage, sadomasochism, and male domination come to equal "liberation" and "freedom"? They don't. And yet these things are now celebrated, promoted, and accepted.

In real life our oversexualized culture has led to the continual oversexualization of girls and women, along with increased violence. Author and pornography expert Professor Robert Jensen of the University of Texas sees pornography becoming "more overtly degrading and cruel to women."[20] He is very worried about the current trend, and you should be too.

> I've talked to young men for instance who have seen so much aggressive pornography that their understanding of what rape is, is from my point of view, extremely distorted. In other words, you will find young men who will acknowledge that they've engaged in acts that meet the legal definition of sexual assault, but they don't see themselves as having committed a sexual assault.[21]

Currently pornography has an annual worldwide profit into the billions. Movies and books such as *Fifty Shades of Grey* are helping to rapidly increase that bottom line. So are many women, even Christian women, who have jumped on the *Fifty Shades* bandwagon. The *Catechism of the Catholic Church* states that pornography is a grave offense (see *CCC* 2354). It perverts the conjugal act and turns people into objects.

Now is the time to put down the mommy porn and stand up for true faith and feminism by replacing *Fifty Shades of Grey* with God's fifty shades, and then some, of grace and mercy.

Pray softly...

Lord, forgive me if I have treated the evils of such things as pornography or other types of offensive material as mere entertainment. I need your love and guidance to avoid these vices in the future and help the other precious women in my life to do the same.

Facebook Made Me Do It

And lead us not into temptation.
—Matthew 6:13

One doesn't have to exactly be a Madison Avenue advertising whiz to realize how strongly we are impacted by our culture. A perfect example would be how you're spending your time right now: reading this book. You might have seen an ad in a magazine or on a poster in a bookstore, or read about it on a website. Something caught your eye and you went ahead and made a purchase. It was a conscious decision. You probably also would agree that you and your close-knit circle of family friends would be a lot closer if you didn't spend so much time in front of the TV or computer. Here again, though, we're talking about making conscious decisions about media choices. They may not always be good ones, but choices are made.

It's an entirely different story when it comes to the media controlling us without our knowledge or consent. Do you think you're above such media mind control? Facebook doesn't think so, and they proved it. In the summer of 2014, the social media giant made international headlines after admitting it engaged in a psychological experiment with its subscribers as its guinea pigs. They played games with the tone of newsfeeds, sending some subscribers more negative feeds, others more positive ones. As a result those who received more negative information in turn wrote more negative posts about themselves, and the same was true for the subscribers who received the more positive information. When the story broke Facebook received a huge backlash, but as Christopher Glidemeister from the media watchdog group the Parents TV Council explained, the much bigger story got lost in the discussion over Facebook's lack of informed consent.

> By contrast, relatively little attention centered on the actual findings of the study: that media is capable of influencing how its viewers think, feel and react. This is probably because however disturbing Facebook's actions, in fact it was essentially business as usual for the media.[22]

If Facebook can have such an impact with just one experiment, how much more have decades of violent programming, explicit sexual content, and incessant advertising and commercialism had on the way we see the world, live our lives, and relate to God?

Pray softly...

Dear Lord, I never realized how strongly I am most likely affected by the various forms of media that permeate our every waking moment.

Help me become more aware of these influences and give me the strength to spend less time with technology and more time with my family and you.

Eat, Drink, and Be Faithful

*No longer drink only water, but use a little wine for the sake
of your stomach and your frequent ailments.*
—1 TIMOTHY 5:23

Interesting, isn't it? Present day health research about drinking wine in moderation for health reasons is backed up in Scripture. Don't you just love God? OK, seriously, not everybody at the local bistro down the street is drinking Cabernet or Pinot Grigio to cure a stomachache or heartburn. What we're talking about is balance and moderation. On the one hand, in our "supersize me," fast-food world, the idea of self-control too often gets lost. On the other hand some Christians take things to the extreme and not only say *arriverderci* to the vino but *ciao ciao* to having any fun at all. On top of that, they try to make sure no one else around them has any fun either.

And that's what we're talking about here—enjoying life and having fun in a godly way. Your version of enjoyment may or may not come with an occasional glass of wine or an occasional night on the town with your friends. That's fine. But whatever you do, get out there—and do so wearing a smile. How in the world is anyone going to be attracted to Jesus through us if we're constantly starring in our version of *SNL*'s Church Lady?

Pope Francis might not be familiar with *Saturday Night Live*, but according to a daily homily he gave at the Vatican in May 2013, he apparently has run into quite a few Enid Strict types along the way. He compared them to "pickled peppers."

> Sometimes these melancholy Christians faces have more in common with pickled peppers than the joy of having a beautiful life. Joy cannot be held at heel: it must be let go. Joy is a pilgrim virtue. It is a gift that walks, walks on the path of life, that walks with Jesus: preaching, proclaiming Jesus, proclaiming joy, lengthens and widens that path. It is a virtue of the Great, of those Great ones who rise above the little things in life, above human pettiness, of those who will not allow themselves to be dragged into those little things within the community, within the Church: they always look to the horizon.[23]

So eat, drink, (in moderation, of course), be faithful, and be joyful. Look to the horizon and politely say *hasta la vista* to the Church Lady and her band of pickled-peppered Christians.

Pray softly…

Lord, you have given us so much beauty and so many good things to be joyful about it! I pray that I can be a good witness by living out my life with a smile on my face and a real pep in my step as I proclaim and preach about your Son.

The Lady Does Protest Too Little

Open your mouth for the mute,
for the rights of all who are left destitute.
—Proverbs 31:8

I have a stone plaque on my desk with a beautiful Scripture verse carved into it. It was given to me by a listener in Florida during one of my speaking engagements. She thanked me for my work and told me to keep speaking out against the many evils in our world.

I treasure that plaque because it gives me daily encouragement to speak the truth in love as St. Peter reminds us so eloquently in 1 Peter 3:15. But as I told the lovely woman who gave me this gift, those of us with a platform can't do it alone. Today, when a laundry list of ills face our society—wars, persecutions, rampant sexual immorality, broken relationships, just for starters—you can see why it is definitely not an "Oh, I will get to that later" approach that is needed, but a "man (or woman) your battle stations; all hands on deck" battle cry.

You might be thinking, *Who, me? What difference could I possibly make?* Or maybe this little mantra sounds familiar: *I don't have the time.* It's also quite common to think when we're trying to avoid getting involved, *That's what Father, Sister, or Pastor So-and-So is supposed to do.*

That's their job, not mine.

That's not what Jesus says, though. Let me just share with you a few examples concerning what Scripture says is expected of us, if we really say we are Christians.

Heal the sick, raise the dead, cleanse lepers, cast out demons. You received without paying, give without pay." (Matthew 10:8)

Greater love has no man than this, that a man lay down his life for his friends. (John 15:13)

Let each of you look not only to his own interests, but also to the interests of others." (Philippians 2:4)

For I was hungry and you gave me food, I was thirsty and you gave me drink, I was a stranger and you welcomed me, I was naked and you clothed me, I was sick and you visited me, I was in prison and you came to me. (Matthew 25:35–36)

This is just for starters. As you might imagine, there are plenty more where those came from. Call me crazy, but it sounds like this Christianity thing is pretty much a contact sport.

OK, take a deep breath. I am not suggesting that you quit your job, grab a soapbox, and start preaching about Jesus in the middle of Grand Central Station. (I actually have a friend who did feel called to do just that, and now he has a huge Catholic evangelization ministry, but that's clearly not for everybody.) However, being a believer means more than just believing. It means more going to Mass or church services once or twice a week. It might mean grabbing the kids and helping out once a month at the local soup kitchen or crisis pregnancy center. Maybe you have very small children and lending a helping hand outside the home is not feasible. Well, one of the good things about the Internet is that, when it is used wisely, it can make a difference. If there is a particular issue that is near and dear to your heart, you can formulate an editorial and send it off to your favorite newspaper or online news source. Have you ever thought about starting your own blog? Don't forget about Pinterest, Facebook, and Twitter—on more than one occasion these have become outlets for campaigns that have led to positive change and awareness.

St. Teresa of Avila, the great mystic, spiritual writer, and one of four female doctors of the Catholic Church, reminds us that Jesus is counting on all of us to do our part. "In the face of so many enemies it's not possible for us to sit with our hands folded."[24]

Pray softly...

Lord, I know we are called to be your hands and feet. Please show me where I can make a difference in our troubled world. How can my gifts and talents to be used to better serve my brothers and sisters in need?

Love Means Having to Say You're Sorry— and Then Some

When pride comes, then comes disgrace;
but with the humble is wisdom.

—PROVERBS 11:2

Oh, it was so romantic—or so those of us growing up in the 70s thought of the popular film *Love Story*. It's the fictional tale of a young, starry-eyed couple, Oliver and Jennifer. They meet in college, fall madly in love, get married, and after only a few short years together, Jennifer dies of leukemia.

True, the story is very sad. But some of the lines in the movie were not only extremely sappy but downright silly in terms of what is needed to build a strong marriage. It was Jennifer, who, after their first major newlywed fight, utters the most well-known albeit ludicrous line of the film. Oliver finds her sitting outside, sobbing in the freezing cold. He is about to utter the words a spouse longs to hear after an argument. Instead, Jennifer whispers, "Love means never having to say you're sorry." As a Christian and a woman who has been married for over thirty years, my response to that is hogwash, plain and simple.

While it is obvious the lovebirds quickly made up in the movie and their passionate relationship continued where it left off; it's a movie, after all. It's Hollywood, for crying out loud. Not real life.

One of the many issues that caused serious problems in my marriage was the issue of pride along with our inability to calmly sit down and really talk about our disagreements. Not only did both my husband and I have difficulty with the words "I'm sorry," for the longest time the phrases "I was wrong," or "I should have asked you first" were nowhere to be found in our vocabularies. We were too busy keeping score, pointing out each other's faults while ignoring our own, and clinging every so strongly to our egos.

It took God coming back into our lives, after we came close to divorce, in order for us to start waking up and smelling the cappuccino.

As a sister in Christ, let me ask you: is there someone you need to forgive? Is there someone to whom you owe an apology? Remember, love *does* mean saying you're sorry—and a heck of a lot of other things as well.

Pray softly...

Lord, I find it hard to say those few words that mean so much. Please show me how my pride might be causing friction and strife in my relationships, and give me the courage to say what needs to be said.

Faith: It Does a Body Good

A cheerful heart is good medicine,
but a downcast spirit dries up the bones.
—Proverbs 17:22

We're all trying to be healthier these days. It's not an easy task, given our hectic schedules. But I know I feel better when I get to the gym at least a few times a week and steer clear of salty, fatty foods. I also feel better physically, not just emotionally, when I stay close to God and active in my faith. That's not mere coincidence. There is an actual growing amount of evidence showing that faith is good for us on the spiritual *and* physical level.

For example, one study of liver transplant patients conducted a few years ago found that those who were actively "seeking God" were more likely to survive.[25] The researchers interviewed transplant patients and, after two years, found that the patients who had a strong religious connection were three times more likely to survive compared to those with no faith. Similar studies, according to this particular report, have also been done on heart patients, HIV patients, and those on kidney dialysis. Other studies have found that losing faith was bad for a person's health.

A comprehensive report entitled "Health Benefits of Christian Faith" reviewed over 1,200 studies and 400 reviews drawing connections between health and faith. According to this report, published in 2011, faith has a number of positive health benefits including "coping with illness, faster recovery, as well as protection from future illnesses."[26]

But why is there such a strong connection from a medical sense? This report indicates that those who believe in God have a deep sense that it is not all about them.

The report notes that the mental health benefits for believers include: "well-being, happiness and life satisfaction; hope and optimism; purpose and meaning in life; higher self-esteem; better adaptation to bereavement; greater social support and less loneliness; lower rates of depression and faster recovery from depression; lower rates of suicide and fewer positive attitudes towards suicide; less anxiety; less psychosis and fewer psychotic tendencies; lower rates of alcohol and drug abuse; less delinquency and criminal activity; greater marital stability and satisfaction."[27]

It's also impressive to see certain key beliefs of Christianity such as forgiveness and helping others have a positive impact on a number of different ailments. According to the Mayo Clinic, forgiveness is the gift you give yourself.[28] And volunteering has been shown to lower stress levels as well.

The more you give to God and to others, the more benefits you get in return. Sounds like a pretty good deal to me.

Pray softly...

Lord, I am so grateful for all the many gifts you have given me, including my health. Help me to take good care of myself—body, mind, and spirit—so I can continue to give back in your name.

That's Not So Easy for You to Say

Bearing with one another and forgiving one another if one has a grievance against another; as the Lord has forgiven you, so you must also do.
—Colossians 3:13, *NAB*

A few years ago I attended a retreat at a local church. The speaker was presenting a talk on the very sensitive topic of forgiveness. It's never an easy subject to address, and sometimes it makes us squirm in our seats a bit because we probably know there is someone we need to forgive and haven't. We don't quite feel like we have gotten our pound of flesh, so we keep hanging on to the anger and the hurt, thinking somehow this will make that other person pay for what he or she did to us.

The presenter shared a quote that really helped me understand forgiveness at a deeper level. She quoted St. John Paul II who said, "Forgiveness is the opposite of resentment and revenge, not of justice."[29] The minute I heard this quote, my mind went back to 1981 and the shooting of John Paul II in St. Peter's Square. The gunman, Mehmet Ali Agca, was arrested and sent to prison. Not long after he was released from the hospital, the pope went to see Agca in prison, where he forgave him of the crime. Agca didn't walk out of that cell that day arm-in-arm with John Paul II. He served twenty-nine years behind bars in both Italy and Turkey. While St. John Paul II forgave him, a crime was committed and there were consequences to his actions.

John Paul II made that statement about forgiveness more than ten years after being shot in St. Peter's Square. His words were included in his 2002 message released in January, just months after 9/11. He explained how forgiveness is not in opposition with justice; it doesn't mean wrongs must not be righted. He talked about how forgiveness involves the deepest wounds of the human heart, and he said that both justice and forgiveness are necessary for that.

But what if we don't see justice done? That question often comes up. If a grave wrong was committed, we have a duty to seek justice while at the same time exercising forgiveness. If we don't forgive, we are allowing the event to violate us repeatedly, and we are ignoring what God has to say about the subject.

Without forgiveness, there is no real justice for anyone, including yourself.

Pray softly...

Lord, are there grudges I am still holding against someone who has hurt me? Give me the strength to forgive—and be able to receive pardon from you.

His Casa, Your Casa

Contribute to the needs of the saints, practice hospitality.
—ROMANS 12:13

Sometimes all it takes is a welcoming gesture to start someone on the road back to Jesus or into a brand-new relationship with him. You might think you have to have the right Scripture verses at your fingertips at all times. Often the apologist in me wants to reach for the Bible and the *Catechism* at the same time and start quoting left and right in hopes the person will see the light and sign up for the Rite of Christian Initiation of Adults or a Bible study right then and there. Faith is a journey, however, which often begins with an invitation; a sincere gesture showing that someone cares.

A few years ago I was corresponding with a listener who stumbled across my radio show on satellite and began listening with some regularity. She was in her late twenties and lived in New York surrounded, as she described it, by a pretty challenging environment. She was raised Catholic but had been away from the Church and was struggling with a lot of the key teachings. I remember her very first e-mail. She wrote, "I don't want to argue or debate. I just want to understand." She was grateful that I took the time to answer her questions. About two months after we first began corresponding, I was planning to go to a women's conference in New York. Now, New York is a huge city, and I had no idea where she lived in the Big Apple. But I thought, *What the heck*, and threw out an invitation.

At first she was reluctant; she worried that since she hadn't been to Mass in a while she might stand out as the resident heretic. After I assured her that people who attend are all over the map faith-wise and that no one was going to throw stones, she decided to come. The strange thing was that we had never met in person, but the minute she walked up to my booth, I recognized her immediately. We chatted a bit, and she proceeded to go to confession and stayed for the entire event, where she was able to meet some other young women her age.

At the end of the day, she couldn't thank me enough. She felt so welcomed by everyone at the gathering, and it was nothing like she thought it would be. No one was pointing fingers. Everyone was just there sharing their faith and having some great female fellowship. She was pleasantly surprised by the entire experience.

I didn't do any heavy preaching or teaching. I just did my best to answer her questions and be hospitable, because so many Christians had been hospitable to me on my way home and it made a huge difference. Sometimes less really is more. We plant seeds of love and hospitality and leave the rest to God.

Pray softly...

Lord, today I am going to pray about extending an invitation to someone struggling with his or her faith. Please show me who might need to feel welcomed in your house.

Sticks and Stones May Break My Bones... and E-Mails Can Really Hurt Me

If anyone thinks he is religious, and does not bridle his tongue
but deceives his heart, this man's religion is vain.

—JAMES 1:26

Will someone please tell me what happens to our conscience when we decide to lash out at someone online? Come on, we've all done it. It's so easy to hide behind our iPad or laptop and tell a friend, a colleague, and lots of strangers to take a long walk off a short pier. We are convinced it is the right thing to do. We become smug and tell ourselves it's actually the Christian thing to do because, after all, we're supposed to admonish one another, right? So much so that sometimes we throw every piece of e-mail etiquette out the window. Well, aren't we all that and a bag of chips?

What's even more amazing is that we think our e-mail filled with insults written in capital letters and every color in the crayon box is going to result in fruitful conversation or at least the response we were hoping for. It's not.

"Overestimating the obviousness of one's intentions can lead to insufficient allowances for ambiguities in communication—with occasionally destructive results." So says New York University Professor Justin Kruger. Kruger and his NYU colleagues released a study in 2012 entitled "Egocentrism Over E-Mail: Can We Communicate As Well As We Think?"[30]

The authors found that misunderstandings were commonplace, even between people who knew each other. The senders often were overly confident that they were making their points.

Do we really need a study to tell us that we need to back off before hitting that send button? We have plenty of solid instruction from God as to how words—not just sticks and stones—can hurt you and me.

Pray softly...

Lord, have I been using words as a whipping post and hiding behind technology? Show me how to kindly and constructively express myself.

Here's Your Purse—What's Your Hurry?

Do not be deceived: "Bad company ruins good morals."
—1 Corinthians 15:33

What would happen if your son or daughter started hanging out with the bad boy on the block who is always getting busted for something? Whether it's getting into fights at school or stealing cigarettes at the local convenience store, this teen is always in some sort of hot water. While you might feel sorry for the local bad boy, you also would be concerned about him having an influence on your own child and realize that the best thing to do, at least for the time being, is to put some distance between that teen and your teen. What if God is trying to tell us that we might need to steer clear of the adult version of Tommy or Tammy Double Trouble?

As adults we might think we are too sophisticated to be strongly influenced by those around us. It also might sound odd, even cruel, to just walk away from relationships when we're called to love one another, show hospitality, and do unto others. As difficult as it may seem, however, that could be exactly what God is calling you to do if someone in your life is affecting your behavior in negative ways.

Maybe there is a friend at the office who drinks too much and pressures you regularly to break away from work early and tag along for yet one more happy hour. It could be your single friends who expect you to come over for a girl's night out on the town What about the bachelorette party complete with a male stripper, Jell-O shots, and who knows what else? Come on. We've all been there. OK, maybe not to the seedy bachelorette party. But invited to something similar, I'm sure.

In today's sex-crazed, over-indulgent culture, these are very plausible scenarios and common occurrences. With this kind of toxic environment in mind, it is easy to see how, even though St. Paul writes to us from the first century, his instruction is timeless. Earlier in that same chapter of 1 Corinthians, he tells us not to associate with those who are sexually immoral or engage in other questionable activities. And in 1 Corinthians 15:33, he warns us not to be overly confident in thinking that we are strong enough to withstand temptation.

Shortly I came back to the Church, a long-time friend of mine decided it would be fun to have some friends over for psychic readings and séances. Not only did I not want to hand my hard-earned money over to what were most likely quacks who were nothing more than frustrated actors, I knew enough about my faith to realize I needed to run like crazy in the opposite direction. When I politely refused the invitation, she called me old-fashioned and a religious nut. Since we had been friends for so long, it wasn't easy putting distance between us. But I had to admit, we just didn't have anything in common anymore, and there were much bigger things at stake than lost friendship.

Pray softly...

Being a new creature in you, Lord, means I must be willing to leave behind some old ways and some old friends. I ask you for strength to meet the challenge.

If All the Women Jumped Off a Bridge, Would You Jump, Too?

Be imitators of me, as I am of Christ.
—1 CORINTHIANS 11:1

St. Paul is all about following along as long we're going in the right direction—as in following and imitating Christ as he tried to do. Instead, what do we silly sheep do? We head right for the bridge and leap off, the blind leading the blind. And then we wonder why we're not happy.

This is coming not from some "holier than thou" woman who has one foot outside of a cloistered convent. As I write this, I'm looking back at all the dumb, sheep-like mistakes I made over the years. We've already discussed being influenced by those close to us such as friends or colleagues. But do we ever stop and think how much we've been conditioned by the world—women in particular? I finally did, but it took a long time for the effects of a certain type of feminist Kool-Aid to wear off.

The world, if you listened to the feminist messages in the late 70s and 80s, was all about finding yourself and supposedly living a freer life. Feminists claimed their efforts were designed to remove barriers, including what they perceived as barriers in the bedroom. Bluntly stated, that translated then and now into a "loving the one you're with" mentality. I was influenced by these messages, too. Surprise, surprise, it wasn't very freeing or fulfilling. Unfortunately, however, this attitude of "everybody's doing it" is more common than ever before. Younger and younger women keep taking a long walk off that short pier before diving head first into the murky waters of our culture.

A few years ago, a friend of mine who is a moral theologian was giving a lecture on chastity at a Catholic college. Afterward a young woman approached her, looking half relieved and half miserable. She was a sophomore and, at nineteen years old, had just assumed she was expected to have a number of sexual partners. She was at least expected, she thought, to sleep with her boyfriend, or so she had been thoroughly convinced. Those were the types of signals, messaging, and conditioning she had received over the years. She went along with it because, until she heard my friend's presentation, no one had told this girl anything differently. No one—not her parents, not her educators, and certainly not the media.

It's just another example of why the only people we should be following are those who follow Christ. He jumps. I jump. How about you?

Pray softly...

Lord, let it be you whom I am eager to follow and not the world. I know you have only my best and my eternal interest at heart.

Apparently It Is Rocket Science

*They know nothing, they understand nothing; their eyes are plastered over
so they cannot see, and their minds closed so they cannot understand.*

—ISAIAH 44:18, *NIV*

Dr. Janet Smith is a moral theologian, Vatican consultant, and a
renowned expert concerning the Catholic Church's teachings on sexuality and bioethics. She lectures around the world in addition to her
work at Sacred Heart Major Seminary in Detroit. Whether speaking
in Paris or Peoria, she says her audiences have the same reaction to
her message concerning the benefits of chastity. "I feel like I am going
around the world telling people the sky is blue and the grass is green,
and everyone's reaction is, 'Wow, that is amazing. How come we haven't
heard this before?'"

The truth of what God's plan for us is and what happens when we
go outside of that plan really *is* rocket science for some. It is mind-
boggling because (1) they haven't heard it before, and (2) it goes against
whatever they have been told through television, movies, radio, the
Internet, their friends, educators, and maybe even Mom and Dad. It's
easy to tune into all kinds of voices and frequencies, as Benedict XVI

said, except the voice of God. "We are no longer able to hear God there are too many frequencies filling our ears."[31]

Dr. Miriam Grossman is a psychiatrist that served on the counseling staff at UCLA for twelve years. She explains in her presentations and books that most of her clients were young women in their late teens and early twenties. Thanks to the hook-up culture, the students in her office were struggling with more than just the medical complications from a variety of sexually transmitted infections. She calls it "madness" and says this is why she became an activist working to spread the message about the dangers of the hook-up culture. She said:

> Thousands of kids came to my office. I was alarmed at how many of them had sexually transmitted infections and concerned about students, mostly young women, whose sexual lifestyle placed them at risk for disease, emotional distress and even infertility later in life. These were young people who were otherwise well-informed and proactive about their health. They were careful about what they ate, they exercised, avoided tobacco, and so on. But in this one area, in their sexual behavior, they took alarming risks.[32]

Dr. Grossman saw a great deal of anxiety and depression among her young female patients. That's because intimate behavior results in feelings of attachment for women, even among strangers due to a brain chemical called oxytocin. Stop the presses! Think about that for a second. Given how much society accepts and promotes sex outside of marriage and how much it is actually now considered "normal" in today's world, do we have any idea of all the emotional baggage women are carrying around? We are absolutely not designed to sleep around, and yet that is exactly what so many women today are doing.

Despite what those reruns of *Sex and the City* and *Friends* are telling us, sleeping around is not wise. What seems like rocket science is really nothing more than common sense.

Pray softly...

Dear God, open my eyes, my mind, and most importantly my heart so I can see where I may have been misled and betrayed by voices other than yours. Help me to learn to listen to the wisdom of your Holy Spirit.

Let Your Head Rule Your Heart

For which of you, desiring to build a tower, does not first sit down and count the cost, whether he has enough to complete it?

—LUKE 14:28

At first glance this Scripture verse seems as if Jesus is bursting our bubble. If we have a dream of doing great things, shouldn't we just go for it? Our heart is supposed to rule our head because that is where the real desire and passion comes from. This is America, the land of the free and the home of the brave, where we can "shoot for the stars" but also "lasso the moon." And what about the tiny mustard seed of faith? Jesus said that's all it takes to move mountains, right?

It might sound conflicting, but Jesus's statements in the Gospel of St. Luke might be better understood through another popular phrase: "You can do anything you set your mind to." In these verses Jesus is talking about the cost of discipleship. God gave us more than just feelings and emotions. Jesus is reminding us that there is too much at stake to allow those emotions take over the steering wheel. In Luke 14:29–31, Jesus continues teaching the importance of counting the cost:

> Otherwise, when he has laid a foundation, and is not able to finish, all who see it begin to mock him, saying, "This man

began to build, and was not able to finish." Or what king, going to encounter another king in war, will not sit down first and take counsel whether he is able with ten thousand to meet him who comes against him with twenty thousand?

We greatly admire the superstar witnesses of our day, such as the foundress of EWTN, Mother Angelica, or popular televangelist Joyce Meyer. By their own admission, these two ladies are emotional. They are filled with zeal and passion for the Lord, quite feisty (even hot-headed at times). But they also have a lot of common sense and determination. How many of us would be willing to work as long and as hard as they did to make things happen? It took years of pouring their passion into prayer, planning, and fund-raising, to build their ministries. EWTN is now the largest religious media network in the world, beaming God's word and the truth of the Catholic faith into 148 million homes in 144 countries. Joyce Meyer is one of the most well-known Protestant preachers, with a worldwide outreach that includes countless faith-based books, Bible studies, and daily TV and radio broadcasts.

Whatever dreams we have, whatever we believe we are called to do with our lives, we are to do it all for the glory of God. However, if we are ruled by our emotions, we might fall flat on our faces, and we run the risk of causing others to stumble, too. Count the cost!

Pray softly...

Jesus, please help me understand the cost of doing your will. Help me see how my greatest strengths and passions can also be my greatest weaknesses if I let emotions get the best of me.

Yes, He Can Hear You Now!

When the righteous cry for help, the Lord hears,
and delivers them out of all their troubles.
—PSALM 34:17

It was one of those times in my life when I was just about ready to throw in the towel. It was a combination of extremely frustrating events occurring all at once that made me wonder if I was meant to stay in Catholic media. I'll spare you the gory details, but suffice it to say, it was during a major election, and no matter how hard I tried, I just couldn't seem to make anyone happy. One day I was labeled too conservative by some listeners. Other days an entirely different group of people accused me of being too left of center. Being on the speaking circuit that year was extremely trying, as I never knew what would set someone in the audience off. Nobody was pleased, including yours truly. *Maybe this wasn't for me. Maybe I should go back to the secular media or into public relations work.* My head was spinning, and if I were able to sing I would have belted out on-air my own version of "Nobody Knows the Trouble I've Seen."

After a particularly difficult week, I was grateful when the weekend rolled around and was looking forward to going to Mass with my husband. As we sat there in church, I just poured my heart out, asking God to give me some sort of a sign if he wanted me to stick with this Catholic evangelization thing. I prayed even harder after receiving Holy Communion. As the saying goes, be careful what you wish for—sometimes the Lord will, as my good friend Fr. Scott Courtney often reminds me, "give you a holy two-by-four right upside the head." And that is exactly what happened.

Mass ended, and we headed out to the parking lot. I wasn't actually thinking I was going to get an answer right then and there. But I felt reassured that God would show me, as he always had, where he wanted me to be. We got in the car and were just about to leave when one of the ushers came rushing up and knocked on my window.

"Teresa, I have been looking for you for the past few weeks. I have something for you. A woman gave it to me a few weeks ago and personally asked me to pass it on to you," he said, pulling something out of his pocket and handing it to me. It happened to be a small medallion of St. Gabriel. Over the top of the medallion were the words: "St. Gabriel, Patron Saint of Communications." On the bottom were the words radio and television in big, bold, capitalized letters. The piece also contained a beautiful image of St. Gabriel blowing his horn and surrounded by various media images.

My husband gasped; he was well aware of my inner struggle. I fought back tears.

"I think you got your answer, hon'," he said, smiling.

When I asked the usher who the woman was, he shrugged his shoulders and said he had no idea. That was an odd answer from him, since he had been in the parish forever and knew just about everybody. He said he had never seen her before or since that day when she handed him the medallion in the back of the church. She could have been from another parish and had gone to Mass at my church in hopes of bumping into me. Or maybe she was an angel, sent to deliver God's message through another one of his saints. Whatever the case, God heard me loudly and clearly. He orchestrated everything so I would receive that message exactly when I needed to hear it most. That medallion still sits on my desk and I look at it every morning before I head to work.

So if you've ever questioned whether God hears you when you pray, yes, God can hear you—and he hears you right now!

Pray softly...

Lord, sometimes I am really in need of those holy two-by-fours—like right now. I thank you in advance for always listening and answering the pleas of my heart.

A Loony Kind of Love

Where shall I go from your Spirit?
Or where shall I flee from your presence?
If I ascend to heaven, you are there!
If I make my bed in Sheol, you are there! If I take the wings of the morning
and dwell in the uttermost parts of the sea,
even there your hand shall lead me.
—Psalm 139:7–12

We've been examining how important it is not to let ourselves be like dumb sheep easily led to the slaughter. Whether it's the company you keep in person, watch on your TV and computer, hopefully as you've gone through this devotional you've become more aware of some of those hungry animals banging at the door of your heart trying to snatch you from the Lord.

At the same time we need to realize that, no matter how big and bad those nasty critters may be, our God is much bigger than anything they dish out. He is absolutely crazy about us and will stop at nothing to save us. God the Son loved us so much that he gave his own life for our sake.

I tend to find illustrations of God's love just about everywhere, even in cartoons. My husband and I, for example, happen to be big Looney Tunes fans. Maybe we're a bit loony ourselves, but we happen to think Mel Blanc and the other great voices and minds that developed the Looney Tune characters were targeting adults as well as children with their messaging. There are just too many similarities between the characters, their predicaments, and real life.

Take the episodes featuring Sam Sheepdog and Ralph Wolf, for example. Sam, as you might have guessed, is a very good protector of dozens of little sheep. That's his job, and he is always there and ever watchful. Ralph Wolf does his best, using all sorts of clever tricks, to steal and eat the cute little sheep. As I told my husband one lazy Saturday morning when we happened to catch a few Looney Tunes episodes, the sheep are so much like us. They are just grazing away in the field, oblivious to the dangers all around them. You would think that after a few of Ralph's attempts to grab them and turn them into lamb stew, they would wise up a little bit. But no, they just keep grazing and eating. Sounds a little bit too close for comfort doesn't it?

Ralph, as you might have already figured out, is a wolf in sheep's clothing. When that doesn't work, he disguises himself as a bush, moves in, grabs as many sheep as possible, and tries unsuccessfully to head for the hills. He then tries to pull the sheep down through holes in the ground. Ralph is very persistent. He tries all sorts of different scenarios, and Sam thwarts all of his attempts.

Call me crazy (or loony), but there is a strong Christian message to be found here. In addition to the obvious similarities of the shepherd— or in this case the sheepdog guarding his flock—we have the wolf in sheep's clothing trying to think up one scheme after another to eat the unsuspecting little lambs; again, that would be us. The wolf could obviously represent the devil as well as all the temptations of this world that try to take us away from Jesus and lead us into sin—some of the very temptations we've been looking at in this devotional. It's interesting that, no matter how close Ralph comes to swallowing up the sheep, Sam is always right there to take them back and beat the living daylights out of Ralph. See any similarities? Even when we repeatedly get snared by sin, Jesus rescues us, over and over again, and just like Sam Sheepdog is, ready to have one more smackdown with the devil. God is indeed everywhere, and the closer we are to him, the more we will see him represented in the most interesting places.

Pray softly...

Lord, thank you for your willingness to go the distance to protect your flock. Help me realize that you can be found everywhere, and you are always trying to remind me of your love.

Not Just Queen for a Day

You will be a crown of beauty in the hand of the Lord,
and a royal diadem in the hand of your God.

—ISAIAH 62:3

I was college homecoming queen for a day. Well, maybe not for an entire day…maybe more like fifteen minutes. I was in my sophomore year of journalism studies at Central Michigan University. It was homecoming weekend 1978, and my cousin (who had actually won the title) was getting ready to head to the parade. She was a senior and lived in the same dorm as me, and there was a great deal of excitement. We were all tuned to the college radio station, where I served as a newscaster, because the station was covering all the events. As the radio host was discussing the details for the crowning of this year's queen, he got a bit confused. Being that my cousin and I had the same last name, I was suddenly all that, a bag of chips, with a crown to boot. Yes, he announced to the entire world (OK, maybe just the small college town of Mt. Pleasant, Michigan) that yours truly was the new queen. My roommates and I thought it was hysterical. We ran down to my cousin's dorm room. The real queen joined in on the fun and helped my roomies as they grabbed the cape and crown to drape me in all the royal trappings. And just for a few glorious moments, I had the initials H.R.H. before my name.

Although I never won any type of crown—unless you count my friends and family crowning me a royal pain at times—I *am* part of a royal family. We all are. That's how God sees us: as daughters of the King.

"And I will be a father to you, and you shall be my sons and daughters, says the Lord almighty" (2 Corinthians 6:18).

Jesus is the King of kings and Lord of lords. And if you believe yourself to be a part of his family, why wouldn't you see yourself as someone with dignity, complete with a special plan for your life hand-crafted by God?

Right about now, you're probably saying, "Right on, sister! I'm all over that." Right? Well, not so much. We are our own worst enemies when it comes to the self-esteem category, and there's plenty of evidence out there to prove it. Granted, there are a number of influences that factor into low self-esteem, including harassment and bullying, being ignored, or being left out of popular groups. Most of the blame goes to women of all ages taking media messages more seriously than the messages God is trying to send us. Even social media—and who isn't on Facebook these days—plays a role in how we see ourselves, and it's not pretty.

Various surveys over the last couple of years show plastic surgeons have seen an increase in surgical procedure requests, with many patients wanting to change their appearance *because they didn't like the way they looked on Facebook*. So much for concentrating on beauty from the inside out.

God doesn't care how many Facebook friends you have. He's already crowned you queen of his heart. Put that in your royal teacup and let it steep a while.

Pray softly...

Lord, forgive me for not seeing myself as you see me—as a daughter of the King. From now on I will try and look for encouragement from you and not the world.

TGIS:
Thank God It's Sunday!

I was glad when they said to me,
"Let us go to the house of the Lord!
—PSALM 122:1

Have you ever woken up on the weekend and rejoiced? And I'm not talking about rejoicing because you have the day off or indulged in some extra shut-eye. I'm talking about being really grateful for the opportunity to go to Mass or services. Obviously we don't have to wait for the weekend to be with the Lord in our parish or church. But when the people of Christ join together to honor the Sabbath, and when Catholics receive him in the Holy Eucharist, it is worth rejoicing indeed.

In my work as Catholic evangelist, I am privileged to host pilgrimages that allow Christians to follow the footsteps of Jesus, his apostles, and the saints. Most of my trips are to the Holy Land or Italy. These experiences have helped me appreciate not only my Catholic roots, but also the freedom to worship that we still have in the United States. Christians all over the world, and in particular the Middle East and

Far East, are not only restricted from worshipping in their churches, in many cases their churches might not even exist anymore due to persecution from their governments, terrorists groups, or both. We have all seen the pictures of Christians who have been imprisoned or even killed for their beliefs. In 2014 Christians in Iraq were forced to flee their homes like never before. Many of them were tortured and killed, and key Christian cities (such as Mosul) were turned into Christian ghost towns. The story of the young Christian Mom, Meriam Ibrahim, made international news after she was thrown in a Sudanese prison and threatened with death for refusing to denounce her Christian faith. She stayed strong, and after much turmoil and giving birth to her second child in prison, she was freed.

In the United States there are more than 70 million people who identify themselves as Catholics. The percentage of Catholics who attend Mass once a week, however, is about 23 percent, even though weekly Mass attendance is still mandatory. Not too much rejoicing going on here. I know—I used to part of the other 77 percent.

If you haven't been to church in a while, give God another chance. Take one step toward him and see what happens. Don't take for granted what other people are dying for around the world. Instead, rejoice and thank God that you still have a house of worship on your street corner.

Pray softly...

Lord, thank you for the opportunity to worship freely. Let me never take it for granted! Let me never forget the persecution of my Christian brothers and sisters around the world.

You Have His Word on It

And the Word became flesh and dwelt among us.

—John 1:14

"They lie on the table side by side, the Holy Bible and the TV guide." This is the very sobering first two lines of a poem entitled simply "The Bible or the TV Guide." Obviously this poem has been around for a few years, because when was the last time anyone actually had a hard copy of *TV Guide* on his or her coffee table? (Well, my mom does, but she is almost ninety.) Put that aside for a moment, and take a look at what the poet is trying to tell us:

> They lie on the table
> side by side,
> The Holy Bible
> and the TV guide.
> One is well worn
> and cherished with pride,
> Not the Bible
> …but the TV guide.
> As the pages are turned,
> what shall they see?

Oh, what does it matter,
turn on the TV. [33]

Ouch! That hurts. The first time I read this poem, I had visions of myself sitting on the couch and just aimlessly clicking through the channels, while my Bible and devotional were only a few feet away on the kitchen table. My husband and I got into the habit of looking at the daily Mass readings every day before going to work. We still do that each morning. But I have to admit, sometimes I don't pay enough attention. I need to go back to the Scriptures later and see what the Lord wants to say to me. But more times than not, when evening comes, I end up clicking away.

Let's look on the bright side here, though. I know I need to be in God's Word more regularly (and so do you because you are reading this particular devotional). Yay for you—and I mean that sincerely. If this is the first time you're taking a crack at it, keep going. I promise you, God shows up big time. And I want to encourage you to think about going even deeper once you're finished here. Have you ever thought about joining a Bible study? It is one of the best things I ever did in terms of growing in my faith. There are so many different studies available now, especially for Catholics, that weren't there even a few short years ago.

Once you start opening the Scriptures, you will see how a particular reading for that day pertains exactly to what you are going through. My husband and I have experienced this many times over the years. Let me leave you with one such daily Scripture reading story that occurred while I was writing this book.

It was a warm Saturday morning in August, and I had hit somewhat of a writer's block. I was having a tough time understanding what the Lord wanted me to share with you next. At first when my husband said, "Let's do the readings," my first thought was, "I really need to get back in my office and just write," but I stayed. And guess what? There was a particular Scripture that kept coming back to me. I felt the Holy Spirit nudging me to build another chapter around a particular verse that had to do with allowing God to work freely in our lives. Lo and behold, that very verse was the first reading for Mass that day.

Coincidence? I think not. So put down that remote, and pick up the Bible. Good things will happen by staying close to Our Lord in Scripture. After all, you have his word on it.

Pray softly...

Lord, I desire to learn more about you through your Word. I promise to spend more time with you in Scripture more frequently.

The Biggest Winner

For whoever would save his life will lose it,
and whoever loses his life for my sake will find it.
—MATTHEW 16:25

Losing means winning, and not only on a popular reality show. In the Christian world, by losing your life to Christ, you gain eternity without ever seeing the numbers on that scale go up even an ounce. (I'm also told there are no calories in heaven.) Handing your entire life over to someone, though, is a lot more intimidating than going on national television to get yourself back into shape. And that's what keeps a lot of us from making a total commitment to Christ. It just seems too difficult and too costly.

Despite the challenges of losing weight in front of a national audience, the contestants obviously think it's worth it, because they show up and push through the pain. They give up the donuts and hit the gym. If they stick with it, they will not only lose weight, they might also avoid a number of health problems in the future brought on by the extra pounds and the fatty, sugary foods.

That's a good analogy for walking away from your old life and into a new life with Christ. At first you might have a hard time giving up your free time on a Sunday to go to church. Most of us would much rather go to brunch or to the mall. Maybe you are struggling with bigger temptations. Perhaps substance abuse and gambling have found their way into your life. Just like those extra pounds, it's hard to admit that sin is causing all sorts of problems. Eventually, however, you realize that something—or should I say *someone*—has to give if your life is going to improve.

Christ is waiting for you to have the guts to break a sweat. He really does promise us a lot more than what NBC hands over to its weight-loss contestants. Health and wealth are not bad things to try and achieve, but they don't last forever. Eternity with Christ does.

Pray softly...

Lord, I want to go on a spiritual diet and give up the sins that keep me from you. Help me see how losing my life to you is a winning proposition indeed.

Move Over, Rover; TV Is Man's New BFF

Be sober. Be watchful.
—1 PETER 5:8

It's hard to be "sober and watchful" with a TV in every room. Forget about spending quality time with friends and family, not to mention the Lord. Although our minds are turning to mush, Americans would rather spend time alone with their television sets even when mom, dad, and kids are all home together. It might sound like something out of a freaky science fiction film, but TV has now replaced Rover as our new BFF.

An alarming national consumer study released in July 2014 revealed that we have now redefined our relationship with our TV set. We see the TV as less than a means of entertainment and more and more as a *"companion."* According to the survey commissioned by LG Electronics, some 60 percent of American consumers leave their television on all day long, regardless of whether they're actually watching it.

Now the survey results are great news for the electronics industry but bad news for those trying to get closer to God and each other. Take a look at what this survey revealed:

More than one third of Americans (38 percent) turn the TV on as soon as they wake up.

Two thirds (61 percent) fall asleep with the TV on.

Nearly half (45 percent) switch their TV on within fifteen minutes of arriving home.

Some 35 percent their say their relationship with their TV is so strong they would rather watch the same show at the same time as family members—but in a separate room.

Nearly 73 percent leave their TV on for background noise and also leave it on while doing chores.[34]

If you see yourself and a family member in any of these statistics, I would say, "Houston, we have a problem." How sad that we value our favorite shows so much that we will walk away from our loved ones so we won't be bothered or have interruptions! How sad that we would rather have the TV on while we are doing our chores instead of—hey, here's a novel idea—using that time to talk to Jesus?

We simply cannot progress in our relationship with God if we don't back away from that TV set. How can we hear God's voice if our environment is never silent? In the 19th chapter of 1 Kings, God tells the prophet Elijah to stand on a mountain because there he would be visited by the Lord's presence. You can imagine Elijah waiting for God to communicate with him through a powerful sign of nature. Quite the opposite occurred.

> And behold, the Lord passed by, and a great and strong wind tore the mountains, and broke in pieces the rocks before the Lord, but the Lord was not in the wind; and after the wind an earthquake, but the Lord was not in the earthquake; and after the earthquake a fire, but the Lord was not in the fire; and after the fire a still small voice. (1 Kings 19:11–12)

God's presence was a still, small voice, a whisper. Last time I checked there isn't too much whispering or stillness happening on television these days.

It's pretty simple. If you want to hear from God, if you want more God in your life, you need to be more watchful of what you're actually watching.

Pray softly...

Jesus, you mean more to me than the latest episode of my favorite sitcom or talk show. Please give me the strength to spend more time with you and less time with TV.

We've Come a Long Way, Maybe

But the serpent said to the woman, "You will not die."
—GENESIS 3:4

But we *are* dying, to put it bluntly. We bought the lie and now we supposedly liberated women are paying for it with our lives. I am really glad I have regular access to a microphone because if I didn't, I would literally explode. Every time I think about the bill of goods we've been sold, I feel like the enraged anchorman in that famous seen from the 1976 movie *Network*. I want to stand up and shout (and feel free to join in), "I'm mad as hell, and I am not going to take this anymore."

Far too many women still are taking it. We're swallowing all kinds of things that are bad for us, starting with the biggest lie of them all: that sexual activity through unlimited access to contraception equals freedom. Let's take a quick look at the birth control pill. Were you aware that it is a Group I carcinogen? The World Health Organization gave the Pill that dubious distinction back in 2005.[35] That sounds very freeing, doesn't it? Where do we sign up?

Moving right along, let's see what else this ridiculous idea that sex equals liberation has given us. According to the Centers for Disease Control, sexually transmitted diseases are at epidemic proportions in this country, with about twenty million new cases each year.[36] Outside of HIV and AIDS, women are becoming infected with certain STDs, including chlamydia, at much higher rates than men.

The world—and even quite a few women's groups insist that sexual activity spells freedom for women. In addition to sacrificing our personal lives to get into the boardrooms of America, we're also encouraged to get into as many bedrooms as possible, even if it means risking our health. Why isn't anyone protesting the fact that there's no cancer-causing birth control pill for men? As I said, this kind of stuff makes me want to scream. Actually I spend a lot of time screaming at myself—calling myself an idiot for buying into this garbage for years. I swallowed it all (yes, including the pill) for a while.

Then I met Jesus up close and personal, and I realized that he is the biggest feminist who ever walked the earth. He met me right where I was, in my self-absorbed world, and little by little he rocked that world. It was like peeling away the layers of a smelly onion. He removed layer after toxic layer of the culture that I had wrapped myself in. He did the same for the Samaritan woman, the adulterous woman, the women of Bethany, and many other women with whom he came in contact. And he wants to do the same for you; he wants to help you see that you deserve better than continually putting yourself physically, emotionally, and spiritually in harm's way.

We've come a long way in some areas, it's true. At the same time we women have gotten terribly lost. But it's never too late. Jesus is waiting to help us find our way home. And this makes me want to scream for joy.

Pray softly…

Lord, I am tired of the world's definition of freedom. Please show me the way to true freedom in you.

The Family That Plays Together Stays Together

You show me the path of life;
In your presence there is fullness of joy,
in your right hand are pleasures for evermore.

—PSALM 16:11

It was Fr. Patrick Peyton with the Family Rosary Crusade who is attributed with making the phrase "the family that prays together stays together" pretty much a household term in the 1970s. This is still just as true today, starting with marriages. One 2010 study from the University of Virginia found that prayer leads to intimacy and can also help diffuse arguments. W. Bradford Wilcox, a sociology professor and director of the National Marriage Project at the University of Virginia, had this to say:

> It makes sense that those who think about, talk about and practice their beliefs in the home, those who bring home their reflections on their marriage, derive stronger effects from those beliefs, especially compared to those who simply attend church weekly.[37]

In addition to inviting God into our homes, prayer makes a difference because it involves time spent together communicating what is on our hearts. And according to Pope Francis, quality time includes *playing* as well as *praying* together.

Pope Francis was born and raised in Argentina. Much of his ministry was spent in the poor neighborhoods of Buenos Aires where he would see families constantly struggling to provide for their children—struggling so much to make ends meet that actually being with their children was a luxury.

In a July 2014 interview marking the first five hundred days of his pontificate, the pope told the Argentine magazine *Viva* that he truly believed in the importance of a healthy culture of leisure, reading, and enjoying art. He explained he would often talk to young mothers and ask them how often they play with their children. "It was an unexpected question. It is hard. The parents go to work and come back when the children are asleep," he said. [38]

Certainly, given our own economic challenges here in America, we see many households where both parents work. There is also additional pressure in single parent households where moms or dads are trying to do so much more with less. At the same time, however, more often than not, I'm afraid we're replacing family time with time media time. Watching TV in your bedroom while your children are watching a DVD in the family room is not what the Holy Father is talking about.

My father passed away in September of 2010. He is still very much with me because he left me with so many wonderful memories. One memory stands out in particular. Our family had purchased a new Ping-Pong table for the basement. It was a weeknight, and since my homework was done, I went downstairs where my dad was doing some work and asked him if he wanted to play a few quick games. At first he declined, explaining that he had some drawings to review before work the next day. I guess he must have noticed the disappointment in his teen's face, because almost as quickly as he said no, he pushed aside the plans and picked up the paddle. It was just a few simple games of Ping-Pong with my dad, but the memories are with me to this day. What memories are you making with your family these days?

Pray softly...

Today, let me pray...and play! Thank you for reminding me how important it is to enjoy life with my loved ones.

Do as I Do, Not as I Say

Show yourself in all respects a model of good deeds, and in your teaching
show integrity, gravity, and sound speech.
—Titus 2:7

I was never a big folk music fan. I am more of a rhythm-and-blues type girl myself. But my husband enjoys it, and since marriage is a give-and-take, I have heard my share of Harry Chapin songs over the years. Since I am a writer, I do listen closely to lyrics. And the lyrics to Chapin's 1974 hit "Cat's in the Cradle" still serve as a real wake-up call when it comes to the importance of witnessing by actions rather than words. It's the story of a man who is too busy to spend time with his son. He keeps making up excuses, while at the same time promising he and his son will get together the next day, or the day after that.

By the end of the song, however, the situation is reversed. The boy becomes a man and follows his father's bad example. He makes up his own excuses for not visiting his dad while promising to come by soon. The father realizes that his son is a real chip off the old block, and not in a good way.

Jesus tells us we need to let our yes be yes and our no be no. And he says this pretty firmly: "Let what you say be simply 'Yes' or 'No';

anything more than this comes from the Evil One" (Matthew 5:37).

You might be thinking this doesn't apply to you because you keep your word, at least when it comes to your family. But this applies to other relationships besides those involving blood relatives. Maybe there is someone we have hurt by not being strong enough to say yes or no and mean it. Is there a friend you keep promising to have lunch with but have yet to make plans? What does that say to the person sitting next to you at the office if they don't see you following through? Saying one thing and doing another equals a bad example. "Do as I do, not as I say" implies we're making promises we can't keep. And that can have long term and damaging results, particularly for the one making the promises.

Pray softly...

Lord, please help me set a good example by practicing what I preach. Let me say what I mean, and mean what I say.

He Made This Just for You!

The heavens are telling the glory of God;
and the firmament proclaims his handiwork.
Day to day pours forth speech,
and night to night declares knowledge.
There is no speech, nor are there words;
their voice is not heard;
yet their voice goes out through all the earth,
and their words to the end of the world.
—PSALM 19:1–4

Are you in need of a little pick-me-up in terms of being reminded of God's love? Here's an idea: stop whatever it is you're doing and sit down long enough to simply look around. Surely you will see something of God's glory somewhere. How quickly we forget all the beauty in our world—beauty that he created for our benefit and enjoyment. He is God, after all, and he doesn't need to impress himself. "His handiwork" is another way of him saying, "Hello, down there! I love you oodles and bunches. Really and truly I do, and look, I made all of this just for you."

"But I work in a boring office all day." "How can I see the beauty of creation when I am carpooling kids everywhere?" "Where is God in the grocery store?"

Blah, blah, blah, blah, blah. So look out that office window already! Notice anything special? What about the trees, the clouds, the sun, and the flowers? So you're stuck behind the wheel for a while. Oh, the misery of it all! You too can look around as you're driving. How about taking a closer look at the beautiful children he gave you, even if they are driving you nuts and fighting in the back of the van. And the grocery store is full of God's goodness. Maybe shopping for food is not the most exciting thing in the world, but since you have shop anyway, why not make the most it (and I'm not just talking about the free samples)? Wander over to the produce aisle and look at all the varieties of colorful fresh fruits and vegetables. How about just pondering the fact that we have so much wonderful food to choose from? Me, I can't stop thanking God for *Cheez-Its* and good red wine! Indeed, God's glory is everywhere, but if we are not careful, we can walk right by it and not give it a second thought. I doubt if I would ever walk down the snack aisle and miss the *Cheez-Its,* not to mention the vino rosso, but I think you get the point.

About ten years ago my husband and I were vacationing along the coast of North Carolina. One day we wandered into the local town for dinner and discovered a charming mariner's museum. In addition to lots of great information and photographs detailing the area's nautical history, there was also a section with various exhibits pertaining to the natural beauty of the coastline. In the middle of the room I saw a case filled with about three- or four-dozen lovely seashells. There was a brief summary explaining that each of the shells was actually a particular type of shell with unique colors and shapes.

But what really struck me was the last line in the description saying this was an extremely small sample of the unique, intricate shells found along the nearby shore. I got choked up just thinking about the overwhelming glory of God and the lengths he goes through to provide us with such magnificent detail. That case of shells was just one small example on one stretch of coastline in one part of one state! It's mind-boggling.

So the next time you're feeling blue, put that chin up and look around. Remember God made everything just for you and for me—including all of those lovely little seashells by the seashore.

Pray softly...

Lord, I promise today to appreciate your glory wherever I am. Thank you for making so much for me to appreciate and enjoy!

One Size Doesn't Fit All

*Do not think I have come to bring peace on the earth; I have not
come to bring peace, but a sword. For I have come to set a man against
his father, and a daughter against her mother, and a
daughter-in-law against her mother-in-law.*

—Matthew 10:34–35

There is a lot to love when it comes to those "one size fits all" clothing
items. A few years ago, for example, I bought the greatest one-size-fits-
all black poncho. It's my go-to item year around. It's comfortable. It
makes me feel sophisticated. It goes with everything. It keeps the chill
away in a variety of social settings. It is easy to mix it with all kinds of
other outfits.

Some people try to treat the subject of God like that as well. A one-
size-fits-all religion is comfy cozy because it doesn't make anyone
uncomfortable—namely you or me. These days it is very politically
correct to have a one-size-fits-all "spirituality." We don't realize how
much we actually sound like Barney the dinosaur: "I love you. You love
me." And yet we feel sophisticated and part of the cocktail party crowd
because we're getting along with everyone as opposed to getting the
cold shoulder. No worries about getting any finger-pointing from the
PC fashion police with a one-size-fits-all look going on. But mention

you're a committed Christian—or, heaven forbid, a committed Catholic Christian—and you will be kicked to the curb in no time flat, pretty poncho and all.

In our journey back to the Catholic Church, it was my husband who returned first. Back then I was just fine with the one-size-fits-all faith. You know—whatever you believe or I believe is fine as long as we all get along. However, I soon realized that a real relationship with Jesus required commitment. That translated into not only getting back to receiving the sacraments regularly but embracing all the Church's teachings, instead of just trying a few of them on for size when I felt like it. That made me uncomfortable, to say the least. Why couldn't we just stay in our very chic, noncommittal, comfortable Christian clothes?

But Jesus is clear that while the one-size-fits-all approach might work in terms of our wardrobe, it's not a good look for us when it comes to the Christian faith; it just doesn't fit. The closer you get to the Lord, the tighter the squeeze you are going to feel. Jesus doesn't say he is "a way." He says he is "the way, the truth, and the life."

Pray softly...

Dear Lord, we know you came to comfort the afflicted and afflict the comfortable. Help me get serious about my faith, even if it means throwing away an easy-to-wear version of Christianity.

Give It a Test Already!

But test everything; Hold fast what is good,
abstain from every form of evil.
—1 THESSALONIANS 5:21

"But I heard it on the news, so it has to be true." If I had a dime for every time I have heard that line, I would be a very rich woman. Usually I hear this from listeners who panic because some media source has decided the Church or the pope has done this, that, or the other thing. What it so utterly amazing to me is that, given all the resources we have at our fingertips to do just as St. Paul is suggesting in the above verse, Americans by and large simply accept what they see on the evening news or read in the paper as the real deal again and again.

For example, during the summer of 2013, a number of my radio followers were practically ready to fly to Rome and march on the Vatican because they were convinced that Pope Francis had changed the Church teaching on marriage. Do the words "Who am I to judge?" ring a bell? First of all, the pope can't change core teachings, and Catholics should know better. For two thousand years, the Church has taught that marriage is established by God himself so, to paraphrase Billy Joel, we're not going to go changing any time soon to please anybody.

Secondly the pope, during that now famous in-flight press conference, was not even discussing the issue of marriage. He was answering a question about an alleged homosexual lobby in the Vatican. Regarding those dealing with same sex attraction, the pope actually quoted the *Catechism of the Catholic Church,* explaining that we are all called to be chaste and that, in the end, it is God who judges the heart. The Church uses the word *judgment* to mean a person's soul or salvation. To the world, however, not judging translates into license. Somehow the press missed the *Catechism* reference, not to mention the other statements the pope made about how the Blessed Mother is more important than the apostles and how we need a deeper theology of women. Those statements just didn't fit into the media's image of an archaic, misogynistic institution, so they end up on the editing floor.

With a touch of a button, those wanting to know the whole truth and nothing but could have easily tested every word of what the pope said that day. The entire transcript from the pope's eighty-minute press conference was quickly posted on a number of websites, including the Vatican's. Adults spend about four to five hours a day with various forms of media. Testing everything should be a no-brainer.

Pray softly...

Lord, from now instead of panicking, I promise I will do my homework—especially when it comes to reports concerning you and your Church.

As God Is My Witness, I'll Never Go Shopping Again (Whoever Dies with the Most Toys Loses)

"Go, sell what you have, and give to the poor, and you will have treasure in heaven; and come, follow me." At that saying his countenance fell, and he went away sorrowful; for he had great possessions.
—MARK 10:21

I never met a mall I didn't like. My husband tells me that I will never be granted the gift of bilocation because I would use it to try and shop in two places at once. That's why the story of the rich young man is one that hits home for me. We are living in a material world and—if you're at all like me, a girl who sometimes has a hard time saying "no" when it comes to stuff—that can be a problem. I've gotten much better over the years. But it is still a challenge, namely because I am a public person and it is important for me to dress nicely. It's easy for me to make an excuse for just one more shopping trip. That's why I need a reminder every now and then. A nice, firm kick in the pants on this topic came to me in the form a homily given by Pope Francis at a special Mass in St. Peter's Square in September of 2013.

> Whenever material things, money, worldliness, become the centre of our lives, they take hold of us, they possess us; we lose our very identity as human beings.[39]

The pope's message came at the end of an international conference for catechists. He reminded those gathered in the square that we were designed by God—not Prada, Guess, or Vera Wang.

> The human person is made 'in the image and likeness of God, not in the image and likeness of material objects, not in that of idols.'
>
> Too much concern for material things can lead us to 'lose the memory of God.' With this forgetfulness, Christians 'become empty; like the rich man in the Gospel, we no longer have a face!'[40]

This exchange between Jesus and the rich young man is also telling us that we can't hold on to anything too tightly in this world that might be a barrier between us and God. No, you can't take it with you. Whether it's possessions, money, or those well-thought-out plans for your life, when was the last time you saw a U-Haul being pulled by a hearse?

Pray softly...

God, as challenging as it may be, my desire is to be less like the rich young man and more like a disciple who is willing to say "yes" to you and "no" to those earthly things I will leave behind one day.

The Dog Days of Marriage

I am God Almighty; be fruitful and multiply.
—Genesis 35:11

There's not too much fruitfulness going on in marriages these days. As a matter of fact, some say the birthrates are going to the dogs. Birthrates in the United States, Italy, and elsewhere are dropping dramatically, mostly by choice. This topic caused quite the media and Internet buzz after a controversial *Time* magazine cover story, "The Childfree Life: When Having It All Means Not Having Children," published in 2014. This article should give us some food for thought as well. As St. John Paul II said, "As the family goes, so goes the nation and the whole world in which we live."[41]

> The birthrate in the U.S. is the lowest in recorded American history. From 2007 to 2011, the fertility rate declined 9%. A 2010 Pew Research report showed that childlessness has risen across all racial and ethnic groups, adding up to about 1 in 5 American women who end their childbearing years maternity-free, compared with 1 in 10 in the 1970s.[42]

Pope Francis added to the already heated discussion a few months later by lamenting that too frequently he sees husbands and wives substituting pets for children. Speaking to couples at the Vatican, he spoke of the importance of faithfulness, perseverance, and fertility in marriage.

> You can go explore the world, go on holiday, you can have a villa in the countryside, you can be care-free…it might be better—more comfortable—to have a dog, two cats, and the love goes to the two cats and the dog. Is this true or is this not? Have you seen it? Then, in the end this marriage comes to old age in solitude, with the bitterness of loneliness.[43]

Now before you go marching off to St. Peter's Square chanting "Get your rosaries off my ovaries," take a breath and try and understand what the Holy Father was getting at. The pope wasn't trying to tell all married couples they need to go out and have ten children. The Church teaches that married couples must be open to life. If they are unable to be fruitful on their own, the *Catechism* explains, they are encouraged to adopt or serve the Church in other ways (see *CCC* 1654). Instead, the pope was raising some red flags over a lack of selfless love he is seeing among married couples today—the type of love that is needed for a marriage to survive over the long haul. He is concerned that they have been influenced by a "culture of well-being."

Married life must be persevering, because otherwise love cannot go forward. Perseverance in love, in good times and in difficult times, when there are problems: problems with the children, economic problems.[44]

Given that marriage requires so much self-sacrifice, what will happen for these couples when things don't go so well?

Pray softly...

Lord, please show me how to be more fruitful in my marriage. Show me where I might be clinging to a "culture of well-being."

Wake Up and Make the Coffee

*Go therefore and make disciples of all nations, baptizing them in the name
of the Father, and of the Son, and of the Holy Spirit, teaching them to
observe all that I have commanded you.*

—MATTHEW 28:19

God doesn't call the qualified. He qualifies the called. And if there is
something that has been on your heart for a while, then maybe God is
calling you.

We've already seen how some people have turned misery or suffering
into a ministry. That's one way to make the coffee. But there are plenty
of people who want something more for themselves and their fellow
parishioners and just start doing it.

In my archdiocese, the Archdiocese of Detroit, there is a beautiful
ministry called Awaken (www.awakenministry.org). It combines praise
and worship, Eucharistic Adoration, the proclamation of the gospel,
and a motivational talk—all designed to bring Catholics closer to Jesus
and his presence in the Blessed Sacrament.

It's completely volunteer-based, surviving on donations. It all began
when Maureen Dierkes attended a powerful conference at Franciscan
University in Steubenville, Ohio. She was deeply moved by the joy

and excitement expressed by the students at praise and worship events. They just seemed to be so excited about their faith, and they weren't shy about showing that exuberance even during Mass. She found herself telling God, "It sure would be nice if I could experience this kind of worship all the time." Just as she expressed those thoughts she felt the Lord telling her not only could she experience it, but she could make the experience available to others.

And that is exactly what she did. Awaken Ministry, according to its website, is now a monthly outreach hosted in Catholic parishes. The outreach has become so popular they are booking events at local parishes six months to a year in advance.

Maureen felt, or we could say smelled, a need. She prayed, and then she prayed some more. Little by little the pieces of the ministry came together as God provided the musicians and technicians needed to make her prayer a reality.

Waking up and smelling the coffee means that we are at least aware of the needs around us. Making the coffee turns that awareness into action.

Pray softly...

Lord, I want to do more than just recognize a need. I want to address it by becoming a part of the New Evangelization. Please show me how.

Now That I Don't Have Your Attention...

Let your eyes look directly forward,
and your gaze be straight before you.
—Proverbs 4:25

Has this ever happened to you: You walk out of your office into another room, but when you get there, you can't remember why or what you were looking for? This next scenario happens way too often in my household. I get dinner started, only to have the phone ring in the middle of slicing, dicing, and sautéing. I start chatting away, forgetting about the pot on the stove, and then before I know it, dinner has literally gone up in smoke. Welcome to the world of our shortened attention spans, which, by the way, are getting even shorter.

Ten years ago our attention span was at about twelve minutes long. Now it's down to five minutes, believe it or not. We have become an impatient people. On websites, a delay in page load times can result in significantly fewer views. A study in Great Britain found that the average person switches between electronic devices 21 times an hour.[45]

It's one thing to have attention issues when it comes to completing responsibilities at home and the office. But remember, our first responsibility is to God. We are supposed to love him with our all of our heart, mind, and strength. The result of not being able to pay attention to him could result in something much more serious than burnt burgers or a nasty note from the boss. This is eternity we're talking about here.

So what is a thoroughly modern, twenty-first century, multitasking woman to do? How are we supposed handle everything on our plate, plus work on our relationship with God without getting at least a little bit overwhelmed and distracted? We should do what Jesus did: one thing at a time. OK. Take a deep breath. I know that may sound really radical, but Jesus is God, after all. It might be a good idea to try and emulate him—that is, if we can pay attention long enough to read even a few passages in the Bible. When we read the Gospels, we see Jesus giving people his undivided attention. Whether it was the Samaritan woman, St. Peter, or those annoying Pharisees and Sadducees, Jesus was in the moment. Remember what he told Martha when she was getting all rattled by her sister sitting at the Lord's feet rather than helping make the hummus and tabbouleh?

But Martha was distracted by all the preparations that had to be made. She came to him and asked, "Lord, do you not care that my sister has left me to serve alone? Tell her to help me!"

But the Lord answered her, "Martha, Martha, you are anxious and troubled about many things; one thing is needful.

Mary has chosen the good portion, which shall not be taken away from her." (Luke 10:42)

Mary was not trying to get away from cooking or doing the dishes, despite what her sister may have thought. Martha was trying to be the hostess with the mostest and at the same time maybe keep an ear on the conversation. It didn't work. Mary had the right idea. She made a concerted effort to sit and listen to what the Lord had to say. For most of us, our brains really do turn pretty much to mush when we try to juggle too many things in the air at once. It's a recipe for turning into Marthas by losing our focus and then our tempers.

Time with the Lord deserves our undivided attention. Dinner, the phone, and the office can wait.

Pray softly…

Lord, show me how to be more like Mary and less like Martha. I long to sit at your feet and really hear what you have to say.

You Can Go Home Again

For this my son was dead, and is alive again; he was lost, and is found.
—LUKE 15:24

Thank goodness Thomas Wolfe isn't God. Wolfe authored *You Can't Go Home Again,* which was published posthumously in 1940. The novel is about a man who was rejected and even threatened by family and friends after he writes a book about his hometown. The book is a huge success, but the townsfolk don't like the way he portrayed them so they give him the cold shoulder, toss a few death threats his way, and basically tell him to hit the road. The title of the book eventually became a popular American cliché. It's normally used when someone leaves home and returns to find they no longer fit in or feel welcomed.

Although we may have experienced a similar type of rejection from someone close to us, God's door is always open. What is even more powerful about the illustration of God's love that Jesus gives us in the story of the prodigal son is how the Father gets one glimpse of his son in the distance and literally runs toward him with open arms. Not the type of reception his son was expecting. Before he left home, he had demanded his inheritance money. Then he took off and went on a wild spending and sinning spree. After losing everything and being reduced to feeding pigs in order to survive, he figured it was time to suck it up and head back to the family farm. He planned to apologize and take his place with the lowly servants as a way to pay back his father.

> But while he was yet at a distance, his father saw him and had compassion, and ran and embraced him and kissed him. (Luke 15:20)

As if that wasn't enough, the father decides to throw a huge party for his long lost son and throws in beautiful robes, rings, and some new shoes to boot.

This is exactly what God does for us. If we have a contrite heart and are truly sorry for our mistakes, he welcomes us home again. On top of that, he will give us a brand-new start and a much better life than we had before.

I know it sounds too good to be true, but it is absolutely true. Compared to me and my past before coming back to the Church, the prodigal son looks like Mother Cabrini. It is still hard for me to believe that, in addition to saving my marriage and giving me a new life in him, God also entrusted me with a very special mission and media ministry. And if God can do this for me, why not you?

Welcome home.

Pray softly...

Lord, thank you for welcoming me home again, despite how I might have offended you in the past. It feels good to be back in your arms again!

God Uses Cracked Pots

Yet, O Lord, you are our Father;
we are the clay, and you are our potter;
we are all the work of your hand.

—ISAIAH 64:8

There's a beautiful story about an Indian water bearer who is charged with bringing water to her master's home, using two jugs she carries on a long pole. One of the pots is in perfect condition. The other pot is cracked. Every day the water bearer delivers only one-and-a-half pots of water to the master's house due to all the water that spills out along the road through the cracked pot. Over the years the cracked pot becomes increasingly ashamed of its flaws and finally decides to apologize to the water bearer, only to be pleasantly surprised by her response.

> The bearer said to the pot, "Did you notice that there were flowers only on your side of the path, but not on the other pot's side? "That's because I have always known about your flaw, and I took advantage of it. I planted flower seeds on your side of the path, and every day while we walk back from the stream, you've watered them.

For two years I have been able to pick these beautiful flowers to decorate my master's table. Without you being just the way you are, she would not have this beauty to grace her house."[46]

It's interesting to look at the contributions of the two pots. The perfect pot is proud of being able to successfully deliver a full jug of water each day. But its contributions don't go much further than that. The cracked pot, however, is delivering water and beautifying the world around it at the same time. We should also make note of how the cracked pot finally realized its worth. It was willing to admit that it had issues. (Don't we all?) Yet it was in that gesture of humility and a willingness to want something better for its owner that the real attitude adjustment occurred. Only then did the pot realize its uniqueness and worth.

Sometimes we are so busy closely examining our cracks that we fail to realize how God, the great potter, can use those flaws to make a difference in the world. God wants to shape and reshape us to be the best we can be—chips, cracks, and all. But we have to be start by allowing ourselves to be putty in his hands.

Pray softly

Lord, you are indeed the potter. I give you power over my life to mold me into the woman you want me to become, because there is no better place for me than in your loving hands.

Can We Not Talk?

A fool's lips bring strife.

—PROVERBS 18:6

Humorist Erma Bombeck once said that gossip, not baseball, is America's favorite pastime. Given the myriad ways gossip can get around these days and our apparent unquenchable thirst for it, I'd say she was spot on.

The popularity of reality TV has certainly helped fan the gossiping flames. Shows such as *Dance Moms, Real Housewives,* and others are built around a group of supposedly real people, typically women, who apparently have nothing but time on their hands to look at the camera and tell the world who did what to whom and how often. Our response should be a big fat "Who cares?" but that is hardly the case. The ratings of these sorry excuses for television programming are through the roof, which might mean we're imitating the stars on these shows more than we realize. Don't kid yourself into thinking that it's no big deal. It is. In one of his daily homilies in September 2013, Pope Francis said that, for Christians, there is no such thing as innocent gossip; he says gossip is akin to murder. The pope went on to say that those who simply can't find the willpower to be quiet already are hypocrites as well as murderers.[47]

So what does Pope Francis suggest we do when we feel the need to talk about someone behind their back? Instead of picking up the phone, how about getting on our knees?

> Go and pray for him! Go and do penance for her! And then, if it is necessary, speak to that person who may be able to seek remedy for the problem. But don't tell everyone![48]

No pun intended, but need I say more?

Pray softly...

Lord, forgive me if I have offended you by offending another one of your children by my idle gossip. Help me remember that loose lips not only sink ships but souls as well.

Somewhere Over the Hamper

Her children rise up and call her blessed;
her husband also, and he praises her.
—PROVERBS 31:28

If you're a mom who is having a bit of a downer day or a little bit of an identity crisis, hopefully this will remind you how much you matter in the big scheme of things. Just because today you might not be able to see past that pile of dirty clothes doesn't mean that you're not making a difference.

In her essay on motherhood, "When God Created Mothers," writer Erma Bombeck gave us a look at moms through God's eyes. The reflection might be quite a few years old, but it has certainly stood the test of time. As a matter of fact it might even be more relevant today in a world where motherhood is not given the credit it deserves as an honorable, legitimate, and challenging vocation; a world where too often a woman's fertility is looked upon often as a disease. At numerous points during this poignant piece, it's almost as if God were speaking through her. And I think he was. Immediately you are drawn into the conversation between the Lord and one of his angels. God is in his sixth day of creation, scratching his head as he tries to figure out how even he, the Alpha and the Omega, is going to complete this absolute masterpiece that requires so much selfless love.

And God said, "Have you read the specs on this order? She has to be completely washable, but not plastic. Have 180 moveable parts...all replaceable. Run on black coffee and leftovers. Have a lap that disappears when she stands up. A kiss that can cure anything from a broken leg to a disappointed love affair. And six pairs of hands."

The angel shook her head slowly and said, "Six pairs of hands...no way."

"It's not the hands that are causing me problems," God remarked, "it's the three pairs of eyes that mothers have to have."

"That's on the standard model?" asked the angel.

God nodded. "One pair that sees through closed doors when she asks, 'What are you kids doing in there?' when she already knows. Another here in the back of her head that sees what she shouldn't but what she has to know, and of course the ones here in front that can look at a child when he goofs up and say. 'I understand and I love you,' without so much as uttering a word."[49]

While Bombeck was a speaker and humorist, I think she could have also been given the title of theologian. A convert to Catholicism, Bombeck's essay on mothers in many ways sounds like the beautiful words of encouragement from St. John Paul II in his 1995 *Papal Letter to Women.*

> Thank you, *women who are mothers!* You have sheltered human beings within yourselves in a unique experience of joy and travail. This experience makes you become God's own smile upon the newborn child, the one who guides your child's first steps, who helps it to grow, and who is the anchor as the child makes its way along the journey of life.[50]

St. John Paul II refers to you as "God's own smile." One of the most popular contemporary American writers thinks so highly of you that she believes that even the Lord himself might have been stumped when it came time to finish his stunning creation.

So remember, side by side with God, you are having a huge impact on the world; one hug, one homework assignment, one hamper of laundry at a time.

Pray softly...

Lord, thank you for the gift of motherhood, for the privilege of being able to co-create with you. Please give me strength and wisdom to carry out this most precious assignment in guiding my children through life.

Denial Is Not Just a River in Egypt

Training us to renounce irreligion and worldly passions,
and to live sober, upright, and godly lives in this world.
—Titus 2:12

Are you a fan of country music? If so you might remember a really catchy song released by Pam Tillis in 1993 entitled "Cleopatra, Queen of Denial." It's about a woman who ignores all the signs that her boyfriend is really a creep. She buys all his alibis and floats, as the song says, down a river of lies.

How often in my own life did I share in that not-so-royal title? There I was, floating merrily along on my own river of lies. I was kidding myself that my marriage would be just fine even after ignoring it for so many years—all so I could make it to the top of my profession. That's why I can empathize with other woman walking around wearing the same Cleopatra-type tiara. One listener, for example, poured her heart out to me in an e-mail. She revealed that she had found her "true" soul mate. The only problem was that her soul mate had a wife and a family, and she had a husband. Minor details, since according to her, surely "God would understand" because they were "meant to be together." Another listener contacted me about her teen daughter who was struggling with an eating disorder. Her mother, however, was in such denial that she referred to her daughter's severe anorexia as "extreme dieting," even though her daughter had all the classic symptoms and had been hospitalized more than once.

I don't think these women wanted advice. They didn't seem pleased when I passed on counseling information rather than personal opinion or affirmation. Deep down I think they were hoping for both affirmation and justification. That way they wouldn't have to do the really hard work necessary to deal with some pretty tough issues—especially if a Catholic talk show host told them to keep calm and Cleopatra on.

Whether it is infidelity, an eating disorder, or a gambling or porn addiction, denial is not going to make serious issues disappear. You have to be willing to face them; you have to be courageous enough to kick Cleopatra out of that riverboat so God can come in and help you head safely back to shore.

Pray softly...

Lord, it feels like I have been floating down the river of denial for far too long. Please take over and steer me in the right direction.

Serious Assembly Required

He heals the brokenhearted and binds up their wounds.
—PSALM 147:3

One of my favorite Christmas gifts I can ever remember receiving as a child was a dollhouse. This wasn't your typical Victorian-like wooden structure with the two floors and a staircase in the middle. This was a lot more complicated to assemble. It was a modern ranch house made of aluminum. It was one story with a variety of rooms and hallways throughout and more pieces than we could count. It was very much in the bold contemporary styles of the day, and I couldn't wait to start playing with it.

My father was a very talented mechanical engineer. He was all about the details, and he was very good at fixing and assembling things. He had no problem helping to design the mechanical systems for a major hospital or office building, but that Christmas morning, a normally very patient man was getting increasingly frustrated by the minute with my store-bought aluminum doll house. He sat there on the floor for what seemed a very long time, surrounded by countless miniature window frames, doors, wall structures, and pages of directions with a very perplexed look at his face.

Finally my mom couldn't take it anymore. It was time to start getting ready for dinner, and she had just about had it with my dad and his Frank Lloyd Wright imitation. She told my dad to close up shop. I would just have to wait until after the Christmas holiday for him to put my dream dollhouse together. That way my father could call the manufacturer and ask for some obviously badly needed help.

Sometimes we are like that in our relationship with God. We think we can handle things just fine on our own. Despite how much of our life may be strewn across the living room floor, we are convinced that, because of our education, our intelligence, and our bloated egos, we don't need any direction or guidance. We like to convince ourselves that we know what's best and don't need any type of instructions even when they are being freely offered to us as part of the package.

But just like my dad's realization that he needed to place a call to the manufacturer, we have to be willing to swallow our pride also and call on our maker: God. People are much more complicated and much more important than tin dollhouses. The assembly process goes on continuously. Lucky for us, our manufacturer doesn't keep holiday hours. He is available for instruction 24/7. We just have to be willing to pick up that help hotline.

Pray softly...

Lord, you know me better than I know myself. Encourage me to tap into your overflowing love and guidance daily.

Little Prayers Mean a Lot

Pray at all times in the Spirit, with all prayer and supplication.
—Ephesians 6:18

Apparently praying in public is a much bigger deal than many of us realize. My husband and I discovered this recently during dinner at a local restaurant. We always try to remember to say grace before meals, whether at home or dining out. On one particular evening, as we were getting ready to the pay the bill, a woman who was dining nearby with her husband began to walk toward our table. Immediately I thought she was going to tell me I had a piece of cheese or something hanging from my chin. Instead she smiled and thanked us for praying.

"I can't tell you how nice it is to see people actually honoring God in public. Our country needs so much prayer these days. Thank you," she said, and then walked away.

Wow. My husband and I were pleasantly surprised. I mean we weren't exactly standing on our table in the middle of the trattoria reciting the Beatitudes or the Ten Commandments. We didn't break out into a big praise and worship number right then and there. We merely said our traditional Catholic blessing. You know, the short and sweet "Bless us, O Lord, and these thy gifts, which we are about to receive from thy bounty, through Christ our Lord. Amen." We made the Sign of the Cross and started to enjoy our meal. It has become such a part of our daily routine that we don't think about it that much. And yet that short, sweet, traditional prayer of thanksgiving in public had made an impact.

This should give us some indication of just how hungry the world is for goodness and for God. This should also be a reminder that we don't have to be a televangelist to be a light in the darkness. My spiritual director encouraged me a long time ago to make another small but powerful gesture. Thanks to him, I never pass a Catholic church without making the Sign of the Cross. As Catholics we believe Jesus is present in the Eucharist contained in the church tabernacle. Making the Sign of the Cross acknowledges the real presence of Christ in the church. It's a way of lovingly saying hello to the Lord.

Pope Francis says the Church grows by attraction not proselytizing.[51] In other words, breaking out into Handel's "Hallelujah Chorus" at the mall is probably not a good idea. It might work with a flash mob during the Christmas shopping season, but sharing your faith should not be seen as an over-the-top, in-your-face type of approach that causes most people to grab their children and head as fast as possible to the nearest exit. On the other hand, little outward signs of our inward peace make Christianity very attractive.

Pray softly...

Dear Lord, remind me that even a small outward sign of faith can have a huge impact in today's world. Help me make you and the Christian faith more attractive to those around me.

The Gospel According to Gallup

I am the Lord, and there is no other,
besides me there is no god.
—ISAIAH 45:5

I didn't really mean to eavesdrop. OK, maybe I did. But I am a trained newsperson who now works in Catholic media, remember? I am always on the lookout for good material. On this particular night, I have to say, the conversation taking place behind us at one of our favorite restaurants was certainly interesting. It was also frustrating, but I knew that it was going to find its way into my writing and speaking.

The elderly couple, probably in their seventies, caught my attention because they were openly complaining to each other about what they believed were issues negatively impacting the Church. Apparently they were members of a local parish but had major problems with just about every core teaching of Catholicism. The only time they stopped complaining was to take a sip of wine or a bite of their meal. When they stopped chewing, they continued griping. Even the very popular Pope Francis didn't meet their approval. For them, he was too conservative and taking the Catholic Church in a backward direction. And to top it off, from what I could gather, they felt were perfectly justified in not following the Church's teachings while still attending Mass and receiving the Eucharist. Those who disagreed with them were the extremists and oddballs. Didn't the Church officials read the papers? Didn't the Vatican know about all the polls showing how Catholics think the Church is still in the Dark Ages?

This couple is an example of what has happened to so many Christians who have been sacramentalized but not catechized or evangelized. They look at God and the Church the same way they look at American government. But God does not run a democracy. He runs a kingdom. The pope isn't sitting in Rome studying the Gallup polls and saying, "Gee whiz, we'd better change these teachings that you gave us two thousand years ago, Lord, because these very opinionated American followers of yours think these tenets are way too strict." If that were the case, the teachings would be going in multiple directions every few years simply based on cultural trends. The Church, by the way, is actually well aware of how Catholics feel. The Vatican, along with other branches, even conducted its own assessments in order to get a better handle on how to teach more effectively. The Church also realizes, as Archbishop Fulton Sheen once pointed out, that most Catholics say they don't agree with the teachings because they actually know very little about them.

There are not over a hundred people in the United States who hate the Catholic Church. There are millions, however, who hate what they wrongly believe to be the Catholic Church.[52]

This doesn't mean we simply go along to get along; we are not meant to follow blindly. It does mean we should love God enough to be willing to learn the *why* behind the *what*. In the end he doesn't want your vote. He wants your heart.

Pray softly...

Lord, you are the King of kings. Forgive me if I have treated my faith like a religious cafeteria, picking and choosing what I want to believe and still calling myself one of your followers.

Don't Rain On My Pity Party

God shall wipe away every tear from their eyes, and death shall be no more,
neither shall there be mourning nor crying nor pain any more,
for the former things are passed away.
—REVELATION 21:4

Wipe away every tear? Not if you're Miss or Mrs. Grumpy Pants. If you haven't noticed, misery loves company—and an awful lot of it. It's not that I'm one for ignoring problems. Part of my work as a Catholic evangelist has to do with exposing some of the not-so-nice issues that plague our Church. But I always try to offer solutions and action items as well to remind Christians that we should never lose hope.

Hope, however, does not spring, spurt, or even drip eternal when it comes to the members of the Grumpy Pants clan. They just can't stop singing the blues, and they want everybody around them to join in the chorus. It might be something they don't like about their local parish or diocese, or it might be on a larger scale. Whatever the scope of the matter, no one is ever doing enough (except them, of course), even though all they are doing is whining.

About three years ago I received a scathing e-mail from a listener who was upset because he heard me suggesting, of all things, that fixing everything that is wrong with the Church is not just up to those wearing a collar or those who have a platform. He was offended that I said something more was expected of the people in the pews.

Sorry, but the truth hurts. The Second Vatican Council, I had reminded my listeners, was a call to arms for the laity to work side by side with the hierarchy to rebuild the Church. The Church couldn't have made it more crystal clear when he gave us the document *Lumen Gentium*, the Dogmatic Constitution of the Church.

> It is not only through the sacraments and the ministries of the Church that the Holy Spirit sanctifies and leads the people of God and enriches it with virtues, but, "allotting his gifts to everyone according as He wills, He distributes special graces among the faithful of every rank. By these gifts He makes them fit and ready to undertake the various tasks and offices which contribute toward the renewal and building up of the Church, according to the words of the Apostle: "The manifestation of the Spirit is given to everyone for profit.[53]

So, in other words, nobody gets a pass. Everyone has a job to do. That said, it is easy to understand the frustration. We have more than seventy million people in the United States who identify themselves as Catholic, but only about a third of them attend weekly Mass. Among those who do attend, there are large percentages that know very little about their faith and are in staunch disagreement with the Church on a number of issues. The Church has been teaching for two thousand years, but the lessons were often not handed down at the parish level, or at least not very well. What was taught was much more about *religion* than *relationship*. Combine that with the mass media explosion in the last sixty years and the so-called sexual revolution, and you have the perfect cultural storm.

But just complaining about the obvious is not productive. We have to be willing to rebuild the entire body of Christ by rolling up our sleeves and getting to work, each one of us tackling whatever our particular assignment is. So the next time you get invited to a pity party, do yourself and the Church a big favor—take a rain check.

Pray softly...

Lord, help me steer clear of the Grumpy Pants family today!

Have You Heard the Choir Lately?

Make a joyful noise to the Lord, all the earth;
break forth into joyous song and sing praises.
—PSALM 98:4

"Aren't you just preaching to the choir?" That's a question asked of me quite a bit due to my work in the area of Catholic evangelization. My response always comes in the form of a couple of questions of my own: "When is the last time you have really listened to the choir? Haven't you noticed that they are not exactly singing in tune?"

Thanks to dismal or practically nonexistent catechesis, confusion following Vatican II, and a culture that exchanged traditional morality for an anything goes mentality, Catholics and other Christians were like sitting ducks—easy pickings for the propaganda of the day. We're still dealing with the fallout decades later. It's not exactly news that large numbers of Catholics are in disagreement with the Church on a number of key doctrines, namely the hot button, below-the-belt issues. So technically we're in the choir but we're off-key and in need a lot of practice.

This is where we should see the glass as half full rather than half empty. If the choir is showing up for practice, that's a great start. They keep showing up because deep down they are longing for something more than the camp fire, "Kumbaya" approach they're been hearing for years. It's an approach that has left them empty and looking too much like the rest of the world. The divorce rate among Catholics over the years, for example, has been running neck-and-neck with the numbers in secular society. Nearly 50 percent of marriages in this country still end in divorce.

That's why Catholic radio stations have grown from half a dozen to nearly 350 in just a few short years. That's why Catholic men's and women's conferences across the country are selling out and regularly must move locations to accommodate more and more choir members. These venues are not playing what you would call middle-of-the-road Catholic melodies. This is the hard-hitting truth that sings of leaving behind a cafeteria, milquetoast Catholicism for a fired-up, hands-on faith.

I keep preaching to the choir because I am part of the choir—still growing, still learning, still trying to fine-tune my life for God. So what do you say? Why not grab that songbook and join in? And remember, it's not about singing a perfect song to the Lord; it's singing a joyful one.

Pray softly...

Lord, I may not sing like a bird, but I am praying for the guidance to be more in tune with you and the teachings of your Church.

If God Has Told You Once,
He's Told You a Thousand Times

We love because he first loved us.
—1 JOHN 4:19

Several years ago I was preparing a talk for a women's retreat. I needed a few Scripture verses to help describe God's love for us, so I did a Google search using the words "verses describing God's love." I immediately had more links than I knew what to do with. But something else caught my eye. It was a website with a very special compilation of love verses. It was entitled "The Father's Love Letter" (www.fathersloveletter.com). This compilation paraphrases dozens of verses from the Bible that speak of God's love. The Internet version allows one to click on the verse associated with each line of Scripture. It does a great job of illustrating God's beautiful handiwork in creating each human being, and it's written in a way even the most Biblically illiterate could understand.

On the surface, with so many verses proclaiming God's never-ending love, it might seem to be an easy concept to grasp. All we have to do is read the Bible or look long and hard at a cross or a crucifix. St. Paul tells us in Romans that we can make sense out of losing our lives for a good person, but Jesus died while we were still sinners. And while he was dying on the cross he was forgiving both those who were accusing him and the soldiers carrying out the unjust ruling.

Who does that? Well God, quite frankly.

In my years of talking with women from all age groups, I believe there are quite a few reasons why some might not be able to grasp God's love. Let me highlight just a few of them. Some occur because of women's broken relationships with men, which leads to a lack of trust. According to the Department of Health and Human Services, one in six women "have reported experiencing rape or attempted rape at some time in their lives."[54] The mainstreaming of pornography and the increase in sexual content on TV is also connected to an increase in the sexual objectification of women. Many of us don't feel loved by men; we feel used. Then we have the continual messages telling women that unless they can fit into a 000 jean, they might as well call it a day. And this is just for starters, folks.

Let's not forget that many children in America today can't identify with a father figure because their father is nowhere to be found. Government statistics show that about 40 percent of births in 2012 were out of wedlock.[55] The figure was the highest among African Americans at just over 72 percent, according to the Census Bureau.[56] This is a tragedy, and although no human relationship can ever be a substitute for a relationship with God, we can't expect those who have been abused in some way, those who haven't known unconditional love from a parent or a spouse, to say, "Hey, this Christian thing sounds great. Where do I sign up?" If you're one of those women still struggling with accepting God's love, I get it. More importantly, so does God. Just don't give up on him. Stay with it. Do the Matthew 7:7 thing: Keep asking, seeking, knocking, and watching.

When my husband first came back to the Church, he practically hit me over the head with the Bible and the Catholic *Catechism*. He just didn't get why I didn't get it. It was all right there, in black and white. After a while, though, he backed off, and that's when I really started to pay attention and notice how he was changing. He had so much peace that I wanted at least a little bit of what he had obtained.

Remember, wherever we are at in our relationship with the Lord, we are all called to witness by virtue of our baptism. So walk softly, ladies, and do the best you can, no matter how much baggage you're carrying, to spread the message of Christ's love with every step. If we truly reflect Christ, others will be attracted, not to us, but to him.

In the end, it is Jesus who does the saving. We're just his foot soldiers who happen to be wearing a great pair of shoes.

Pray softly...

Lord, I want to be your hands and feet, and do so with confidence in you and the gifts you've given me. Help me apply what I have learned here to enjoy a happier life with you.

Put Your Best Faith Forward

Although you've come to the end of the book, don't let this mark the end of the inspiration you have received. *Walk Softly* is designed to be your companion as you take one step at a time, putting your best faith forward every day. Hopefully you've realized a few new, fascinating facts about God or have experienced this book as a refresher course—a way of getting reconnected with him.

So how do you apply the insights you've gleaned from these reflections? Here are a few suggestions.

For starters, keep this book with you.

Remember, this is meant to be the go-to devotional for women on the go. And unless you have a photographic memory, given the amount of information that we try to cram into our brains on a daily basis combined with our overloaded schedules, you're probably not going to remember the spiritual tugs or warm fuzzies you hopefully received as you turned the pages. So tuck *Walk Softly* in that great bag of yours, and don't leave home without it. Treat it as you did when you first purchased it; something to go to in the middle of your day when you needed a pick-me-up or a reminder that God really does think you're a rock star and then some.

Write outside the lines, literally.

As you're journeying back through the chapters, grab that pen and highlighter and jot down what pops into your head. If you can remember how you felt when you first began reading, make some notes about your thoughts and emotions. Underline, highlight, circle—whatever floats your boat, as long as you walk away knowing God and yourself a little bit better. If you're having a hard time recalling how you felt when you first took a walk through these pages, go around the block a few more times. Treat it like a good bowl of nice, warm chicken soup. It can't hurt. And the insights you receive the second or third time out the door might be more meaningful as they're revisited.

Ask yourself some questions.

Depending on your state in life, different passages or topics affect each reader differently. That's why it's so good to keep this devotional with you or someplace very accessible. Right now, if you're a young mom, you might find the "Somewhere over the Hamper" or "Necessity Is the Mother of the Microwave" right up your alley—descriptions of life to which you can really relate. Ask yourself specifically why you're drawn to a particular section. What does it mean to you to read that you're not alone, that other women are experiencing similar struggles or emotions?

Take those questions to God in prayer.

If you're a Catholic Christian, find the nearest parish with Eucharistic Adoration and take those same questions to Jesus in the Blessed Sacrament. Make them part of your prayer as you sit in silence before him. Get to Mass a few minutes early and ask the questions again. If you're a Protestant Christian, find a special place that provides some solitude and silence. That may be your local church or it may be in your backyard, on your apartment balcony, or a bench in the park down the street. Just find time to be alone with God and ask those questions. Jesus wasn't kidding when he told us to ask, seek, and knock. He said that, if we asked, the door would be opened.

> Ask, and it will be given you; seek, and you will find; knock and it will be opened to you. For every one who asks receives, and he who seeks finds, and to him who knocks it will be opened. (Matthew 7:7–8)

Ask God to show you how he wants you to apply what you've learned to your daily life. As you go deeper in prayer, trust that God will reward your sincerity with a clearer vision of how to find and fulfill his will for your life. Most likely it won't happen overnight. Don't expect any billboards to drop smack dab in the pew in front of you. But if you keep both your heart and the spiritual lines of communication open, the answers will come to you in a variety of beautiful ways. The more you pray, the more you'll be able to recognize and discern those answers. Sometimes they will be so over-the-top obvious it will make you laugh out loud, and you'll find yourself saying, "OK, I get it!"

Revisit the Scripture passages.

A few years ago my spiritual director advised me to practice *lectio divina* when doing my daily Scripture readings. That's a fancy Latin terms that literally translates into "divine reading." It's a wonderful prayer exercise that can really strengthen your understanding and appreciation of Scripture. Pick a verse and then look it up in the Bible. Read the verses before and after the one you've chosen and slowly go over each word. Place yourself right there in the biblical scene laid out before you and see what type of understanding or clarity comes to you about God's Word. You'll be amazed at how closely you will identify with the men and women who grace the pages of Scripture and blazed the faith trail before you. And you'll be surprised at how many of them will also become walking partners.

Consider Walk Softly your spiritual GPS.

As you ponder what you've learned about yourself and God after reading this devotional, think about how *Walk Softly* might be prompting you to go somewhere you've never gone before—maybe joining a Bible study program, attending a retreat, or going on pilgrimage. Visit the following resource section and really think about exercising those faith muscles. Hopefully you've gleaned some nuggets from this devotional, but remember, if you don't use them, you'll lose them. You might be surprised to learn just how many great resources there are to grow in one's faith. You'll be amazed at how far the Lord will take you, even if right now you're someone who hasn't ventured beyond the front porch.

Just keep walking.

You are unique and special, and that means the feelings, emotions, insights, and spiritual growth you experience will also be unique and special, according to your particular set of circumstances. Don't judge yourself or think less of yourself if your friend starts making a major dash to what seems to be the front of the faith finish line. God is not standing on the sidelines holding some giant stopwatch. He just wants you to take those first steps and keep moving. Everyone is different. And that's OK. So again, just keep walking. Walk softly, slowly, or swiftly, but always in the same direction—toward the open arms of Jesus. Ready. Set. Go!

Suggested Resources

Books

Budziszewski, J. *The Line Through the Heart: Natural Law as Fact, Theory, and Sign of Contradiction.* Wilmington, DE: Intercollegiate Studies Institute; 1st edition, 2011.

DeStefano, Anthony. *A Travel Guide to Heaven.* New York: Image, 2005.

De Wohl, Louis. *Lay Siege to Heaven: A Novel about Saint Catherine of Siena.* San Francisco: Ignatius, 1991.

Hain, Randy. *Joyful Witness: How to Be an Extraordinary Catholic.* Cincinnati: Servant, 2014.

Alexander, Greg and Julie. *Marriage 911: How God Saved Our Marriage and Can Save Yours, Too,* Cincinnati: Servant, 2011.

News

CATHOLIC NEWS AGENCY
www.catholicnewsagency.com
FRANCISCAN MEDIA
www.franciscanmedia.org
VATICAN NEWS
www.news.va

Publications

Living Faith
www.livingfaith.com
Magnificat
www.magnificat.net
National Catholic Register
www.ncregister.com
Our Sunday Visitor
www.osv.com
spiritoffrancis.tumblr.com.
www.stanthonymessenger.org
Word Among Us
www.wordamongus.net

Television/Radio

Ave Maria Radio
www.avemariaradio.net
The Catholic View for Women (EWTN)
www.thecatholicviewforwomen.com
EWTN (Eternal Word Catholic TV Network)
www.ewtn.com

Websites

Catholic Scripture Study International
 www.cssprogram.net
Christlife Lay Catholic Ministry
 www.christlife.org
Couple Prayer
 www.coupleprayer.org
ENDOW: Educating on the Nature and Dignity of Women
 www.endowgroups.org
The Great Adventure Catholic Bible Study
 www.biblestudyforcatholics.com
Integrated Catholic Life
 www.theintegratedcatholiclife.org
National Marriage Encounter
 marriage-encounter.org
Patheos
 www.patheos.com
Retrouvaille
 www.retrouvaille.org
St. Paul Center for Biblical Theology
 www.salvationhistory.com
Symbolon: The Catholic Faith Explained
 www.augustineinstitute.org/symbolon

Notes

1. "Papal Address to Participants in Congress on Women," http://www.zenit.org/en/articles/papal-address-to-participants-in-congress-on-women.
2. Mother Teresa, *Come Be My Light: The Private Writings of the Saint of Calcutta* (New York: Image, 2009), p. 20.
3. Quoted in Bernard McGinn, ed., *The Essential Writings of Christian Mysticism* (New York: Random House, 2006), p. 365.
4. *The Wizard of Oz*, Victor Fleming, director (MGM, 1939).
5. Anne-Marie Slaughter, "Why Women Still Can't Have It All," *The Atlantic*, June 13, 2012.
6. "Giving makes young children happy UBC study suggests," The University of British Columbia, http://news.ubc.ca/2012/06/19/giving-makes-young-children-happy-ubc-study-suggests/.
7. Michael Foust, "Only 46% of children grow up in an intact home, study says," Baptist Press, http://www.bpnews.net/36616.
8. Bootie Cosgrove-Mather, "Single-Parent Kids More At Risk," CBS News, February 4, 2003, http://www.cbsnews.com/news/single-parent-kids-more-at-risk/.
9. "Press Conference of Pope Francis During the Return Flight," Apostolic Journey to Rio de Janeiro on the Occasion of the XXVIII World Youth Day, July 28, 2013, http://w2.vatican.va/content/francesco/en/speeches/2013/july/documents/papa-francesco_20130728_gmg-conferenza-stampa.html.
10. Pope Francis, General Audience, June 11, 2014.
11. "Let God disrupt your plans, Pope Francis teaches," Catholic News Agency, http://www.catholicnewsagency.com/news/let-god-disrupt-your-plans-pope-francis-teaches/.
12. Shaun Dreisbach, "Shocking Body-Image News: 97% of Women Will Be Cruel to Their Bodies Today," *Glamour*, http://www.glamour.com/

health-fitness/2011/02/shocking-body-image-news-97-percent-of-women-will-be-cruel-to-their-bodies-today.

13. Dreisbach.

14. Jackie Willis, "Bethenny Frankel Causes Controversy By Wearing 4-Year-Old Daughter's Pajamas, ET, http://www.etonline.com/news/148356_bethenny_frankel_fits_into_her_4_year_old_daughters_pajamas/.

15. Marianne Mychaskiw, "Report: Women Spend an Average of $15,000 on Makeup in Their Lifetimes, *InStyle*, http://news.instyle.com/2013/04/17/women-makeup-spending-facts/; ABC News Staff, "100 Million Dieters, $20 Billion: The Weight-Loss Industry by the Numbers," http://abcnews.go.com/Health/100-million-dieters-20-billion-weight-loss-industry/story?id=16297197.

16. Quoted in Julie Edelman, *The Ultimate Accidental Housewife: Your Guide to a Clean-Enough House* (New York: Hachette, 2008), chapter seven.

17. Including the website www.emarketer.com, which regularly tracks media usage.

18. Gilbert K. Chesterton, *What's Wrong with the World* (New York: Dodd, Mead, 1912), p. 48.

19. MSNBC interview, March 2013 during papal enclave.

20. Jennifer Bowman, "Researcher links porn to violence against women," http://www.muskokaregion.com/news-story/3579711-researcher-links-porn-to-violence-against-women/.

21. Bowman.

22. Christopher Bildemister, "Facebook Proves Media Influences Users," Parents Television Council, http://w2.parentstv.org/blog/index.php/2014/07/10/facebook-proves-media-influences-users.

23. Deacon Greg Kandra, "Pope Francis on joy: melancholy Christians are like 'pickled peppers,'" http://www.patheos.com/blogs/deaconsbench/2013/05/pope-francis-on-joy-melancholy-christians-are-like-pickled-peppers/.

24. Teresa of Avila, *The Collected Works of Saint Teresa of Avila* (Washington, D.C.: ICS, 1980), p. 223.
25. Andrew Hough, "Having faith 'helps patients live longer,' study suggests," http://www.telegraph.co.uk/health/healthnews/8044586/Having-faith-helps-patients-live-longer-study-suggests.html.
26. Ariel R. Rey, "Report: Christians Live Healthier, Longer," *The Christian Post,* http://www.christianpost.com/news/report-christians-live-healthier-longer-49976/.
27. Rey.
28. Edward T. Creagon, MD, "Forgiveness is a gift you give yourself," April 22, 2010. http://www.mayoclinic.org/healthy-living/stress-management/expert-blog/forgiveness/bgp-20055972
29. John Paul II, Message for World Day of Peace, January 2002. http://www.vatican.va/holy_father/john_paul_ii/messages/peace/documents/hf_jp-ii_mes_20011211_xxxv-world-day-for-peace_en.html.
30. Justin Kruger, et al, "Egocentrism Over E-Mail: Can We Communicate as Well as We Think?," http://faculty.chicagobooth.edu/nicholas.epley/krugeretal05.pdf, p. 934.
31. Ian Fisher, "Pope Warns Against Secularization in Germany, *New York Times,* http://www.nytimes.com/2006/09/10/world/europe/11pope.web.html?pagewanted=print&_r=0.
32. Institute of Marriage and Family Canada, "You're Teaching My Child What?", http://www.imfcanada.org/issues/youre-teaching-my-child-what.
33. "The Holy Bible Or The TV Guide," http://www.seekfind.net/The_Holy_Bible_Or_The_TV_Guide_poem.html#.VDKgeyldV18.
34. "Man's New Best Friend: TV Is A Constant Companion For U.S. Consumers," MarketWatch, http://www.marketwatch.com/story/mans-new-best-friend-tv-is-a-constant-companion-for-us-consumers-2014-07-24.

35. "Carcinogenicity of combined hormonal contraceptives and combined menopausal treatment," World Health Organization, http://www.who.int/reproductivehealth/topics/ageing/cocs_hrt_statement.pdf, p. 1.

36. "STDs Are An Epidemic In The U.S., CDC Warns," MNT, http://www.medicalnewstoday.com/articles/256413.php.

37. H. Brevy Cannon, "Across Races, Couples That Pray Together Are Happier, Study Finds, UVA Today, http://news.virginia.edu/content/across-races-couples-pray-together-are-happier-study-finds.

38. "Pope Gives New Interview Marking 500 Days of Pontificate," Zenit, http://www.zenit.org/en/articles/pope-gives-new-interview-marking-500-days-of-pontificate.

39. "Pope Francis: homily at Mass for Catechists," http://www.news.va/en/news/pope-francis-homily-at-mass-for-catechists.

40. Kerri Lenartowick, "Materialism robs us of our humanity, warns Pope Francis," Catholic News Agency, http://www.catholicnewsagency.com/news/materialism-robs-us-of-our-humanity-warns-pope-francis/.

41. http://www.vatican.va/holy_father/john_paul_ii/homilies/1986/documents/hf_jp-ii_hom_19861130_perth-australia_en.html

42. Lauren Sandler, "Having It All Without Having Children," *Time*, http://time.com/241/having-it-all-without-having-children.

43. Vatican Radio, "Pope Francis at daily Mass on Monday," http://en.radiovaticana.va/news/2014/06/02/pope_francis_at_daily_mass_on_monday/1101287.

44. Vatican Radio, "Pope Francis at daily Mass on Monday."

45. Jennifer Smith, "Proof of our shrinking attention spa: Average person switches between devices 21 times and HOUR," Mail Online, http://www.dailymail.co.uk/news/article-2534163/Proof-shrinking-attention-span-Average-person-switches-devices-21-times-HOUR.html.

46. Quoted in Charles Francis, ed., *Wisdom Well Said* (El Prado, N.M.: Levine Mesa, 2009), pp. 241–242.

47. "Pope: there is no such thing as innocent gossip," News.va, http://www.
news.va/en/news/pope-there-is-no-such-thing-as-innocent-gossip.

48. "Pope: there is no such thing as innocent gossip."

49. Erma Bombeck, *When God Created Mothers* (Riverside, N.J.:
Andrews McMeel, 2005), pp. xxx–20. http://www.amazon.com/
When-Created-Mothers-Erma-Bombeck/dp/0740751085.

50. Letter of Pope John Paul II to Women, 2, http://www.
vatican.va/holy_father/john_paul_ii/letters/documents/
hf_jp-ii_let_29061995_women_en.html.

51. Carol Glatz, "In latest interview, Pope Francis reveals top 10 secrets to
happiness," Catholic News Service, http://www.catholicnews.com/data/
stories/cns/1403144.htm.

52. Fulton Sheen, Preface to *Radio Replies,* http://www.radioreplies.info/vol-
1-preface.php.

53. *Lumen Gentium,* 12.

54. Womenshealth.gov, "Violence Against Women," http://www.womenshealth.
gov/violence-against-women/types-of-violence/sexual-assault-and-abuse.
html.

55. Centers for Disease Control and Prevention, "Unmarried Childbearing,"
http://www.cdc.gov/nchs/fastats/unmarried-childbearing.htm.

56. Jesse Washington, "Blacks struggle with 72 percent unwed mothers rate,"
http://www.nbcnews.com/id/39993685/ns/health-womens_health/t/blacks-
struggle-percent-unwed-mothers-rate/#.VDSNPlfLKko.